Learning in an Electronic World

Computers and the Language Arts Classroom

Toni Downes & Cherryl Fatouros

HEINEMANN
Portsmouth, NH

Heinemann
A division of Reed Elsevier Inc.
361 Hanover Street
Portsmouth, NH 03801-3912
Offices and agents throughout the world.

We would like to thank those who have given their permission to include material in this book.

Cataloging-in-Publication data is on file at the Library of Congress.

First U.S. printing 1996.

Editor: William Varner
Cover design: Darci Mehall
Manufacturing: Elizabeth Valway

Designed by Anne-Marie Rahilly and Jeremy Steele
Edited by Jeremy Steele
Index prepared by Gary Cousins
Photographs by Christopher Simkin
Formatted in 11.5/13.5 StonePrint using Aldus Pagemaker 5.0 Macromedia Freehand 5.0 and Adobe Photoshop 3.0 at the Training and Development Centre

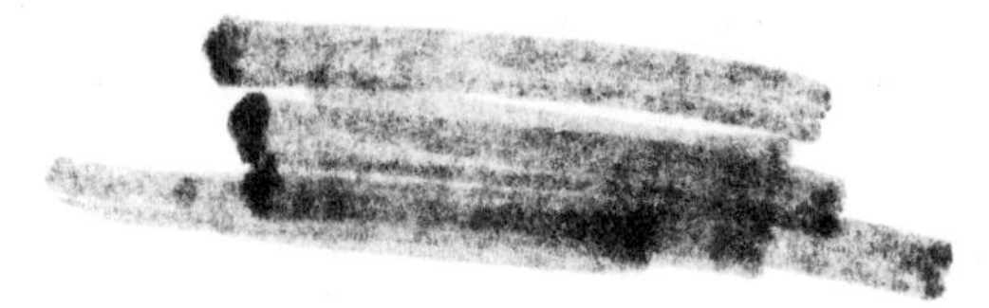

Printed in the United States of America on acid-free paper
98 97 96 EB 1 2 3 4 5 6

CONTENTS

Section One – Changing Classrooms

Section Two – Enhancing Language Learning

Section Three – Moving beyond Print

Acknowledgements

The classroom stories in this book are composite pictures of classrooms where children's language learning has been enhanced by the thoughtful use of computers. The elements of the stories have been gathered during visits and conversations, and by working alongside a range of talented teachers over the last ten years. We would like to thank the following teachers for sharing their expertise and classroom plans and practices with us, as well as for their time and patience in helping us to compile our stories:

Lyn Allsop
Sally Blackwell
Neralie Cavanagh
Lyndel Connell
Margaret Forshaw
Marion Fotheringham
Anne Marie Hutchins
Roberta Janssen
Joanne McDonald
Kathryn Macnamara
Kathryn Orton
Geoff Picker
Jim Porter
Lina Rago
Sharon Sands
Donna Smith
Cheryl Walters
Shelley Wilkins.

We would also like to thank the staff, children and parents at the following schools for their assistance and cooperation:

Hassall Grove Public School
Ingleburn Public School
Macquarie Fields Public School
Menai Public School
Sacred Heart School, Cabramatta
Saint Aloysius Primary School, Cronulla.

To Jan Hancock, we would like to extend our thanks for her valuable feedback on successive drafts; to Henry Legedza, Afrika Taylor, Denise Tolhurst, John Walters, Brian Watson and John Dance Wilson, we extend our thanks for their feedback and advice on specific parts of the text.

We also wish to express our appreciation to:

Sally Blackwell for permission to use excerpts from *In Control: Young Children Learning with Computers*, of which she was a joint author

Karen Robinson, of Innovative Learning, for information about specific software programs

Jeremy Steele for his patience and expertise throughout the editing process

Christopher Simkin for taking the photographs

Christine and Jenni Downes for providing some graphics.

Special thanks also to Michael, Christine, Jenni, Greg and Lee, for their patience and understanding throughout the writing and publishing process.

TD & CF

SECTION ONE

Living and Learning in an Electronic World

Our changing world

Computers and other related technologies have become an integral part of our daily lives. They have altered our sense of people, space and time. From our lounge rooms, now, we can talk to people and watch events unfold in far-off places. Shopping, banking and game playing are just a few of the other daily activities that have also changed. So many aspects of the ways we communicate and handle information have been altered and will continue to be altered by technological development. Cellular phones, answering machines, voice mail, fax machines, cable television, video games, computer networks, satellite communications and e-mail are only the most recent manifestations of change.

Tomorrow's world needs citizens who are able to handle information and communicate using these new technologies. Tomorrow's citizens are today's school children, but unfortunately too few of them are learning in their classrooms how to use recently developed information and communication tools. In most classrooms today literacy is still defined exclusively in terms of paper-based texts. However, concepts of literacy must be broadened to include control over the processes and understandings required to participate effectively in an electronic world.

The development of information-handling technologies

In the past, the technologies for recording, storing, processing and communicating information have been distinct, each with its own history of development. For instance, the technologies for processing number-based information have evolved from sticks and stones, the abacus, Napier's rods, adding machines, Babbage's analytical engines and Jacquard looms to computers. Systems for communicating information have evolved from road systems for messengers, via courier, postal, semaphore, telegraph and telephone systems, to radio, telex, television and fax machines, and today's 'superhighway' of computer networks, the Internet.

Nowadays almost all government, commercial and educational enterprises record, store, process and communicate information electronically, and can do all this within a single system. Electronic databases and communication networks abound. The power of electronic databases lies in the rapidity with which large volumes of data can be sorted, searched and combined. Other issues better handled by electronic management of information include obsolescence (a printed telephone directory is out of date before it's delivered), the sheer quantity of information available, the cost of reproduction and storage, access from remote locations, and the ease of maintaining and using a collection.

The development of language

Language, its uses, forms and related technologies are continually changing too. Technologies of recording language have evolved from inscribed clay tablets and manuscripts written on a variety of materials to printing and mass-produced books, and now to electronic texts. Standard spelling (a technology of writing) is a relatively recent development, prompted by the mass production of written texts. A current example is the standardisation of spelling of the Tetum language, the lingua franca of the East Timorese people, which is now under way as mass-produced books appear for the first time in that language.

Spoken language also continues to change. The advent of mass-produced books (which made mass education possible) contributed to the erosion of many diverse regional dialects and the predominance of smaller numbers of standardised common languages — a process accelerated by radio broadcasting. Today technologies continue to contribute to changes in languages. Satellites combine with television to allow American speech and life styles to enter the homes of many nations, both first- and third-world. Sometimes, however, the trend towards universality is reversed: community-based radio is proving more successful than the written texts of the 1970s as a technology to support the maintenance and extension of Aboriginal languages in the Northern Territory.

The relationships between author and audience have also evolved over time. The traditions of church texts, town criers, minstrels, storytellers, handwritten manuscripts and mass-produced books, as well as particular genres such as choose-your-own-adventure stories, all create different sets of relationships. Similarly, within the electronic media, the advent of video recorders has affected the relationship between the producer, broadcaster and audience. Video audiences can choose their time and manner of viewing (interrupted or straight through) and choose to browse, skip or repeat parts or all of the text.

The effects of these changes are felt by all of us. The newspaper industry is contracting as more and more people turn away from reading to listening and watching for news, current affairs and entertainment. Computer games, television and the telephone have replaced books as the dominant recreational media of many children in the western world (Lieberman, Chaffee & Roberts 1988).

Shifting from the written word to images

One of the most significant results of recent technological change is the increasing importance of images within the processes of handling and communicating information. Multi-modal texts abound in our daily lives, in both print and electronic form. (Multi-modal texts are those which combine at least two of the following modes: spoken, written, non-verbal, visual and auditory. They include comics, magazines, newspapers, signs, posters, television, film and computer systems.)

These texts are increasingly our major source of social information, argument and entertainment. Voters make decisions on what they see and hear rather than what they read — politicians now employ image makers as well as speech writers. Likewise children develop views of the world and themselves more from seeing than reading, and the images they see can powerfully convey cultural values and assumptions. Thus teenage girls today are likely to encounter more images of the 'desirable' female body in a week than their great-grandmothers did in a lifetime.

Changes prompted by computer-based technologies

We've already noted that information-handling and communication technologies have gradually changed over the centuries. The significant differences in today's world are the ever increasing *rate* of change and the enormous *variety* of changes, both of which can be linked to the use of computer-based systems.

A key characteristic of these developments is the convergence of technologies. One example is the combined fax/phone/answering machine and modem (for electronic mail) which has already arrived in family homes. Visual telephones, video conferences and interactive television are also becoming more widely available. The most significant convergence is between telecommunications and multimedia technologies (i.e. those involving images, sounds and written text) — a convergence which is contributing to further changes in the relationship between the language forms and the media that people use. For example:

- The need for elaborate spoken and written language is diminishing as images and sounds are combined with written texts to convey meaning.
- The medium of procedures and explanations, in particular, is changing from print to electronic forms to take advantage of the power of images and sounds. Videos are now becoming commonplace as the medium of instruction for many 'do-it-yourself' kits.
- Oral language may no longer be the dominant form of instantaneous interaction over long distances. Writing can now be interactive and instantaneous through the 'chat mode' on electronic networks.

- Written language may no longer be the dominant form of recorded and delayed communication. Answering machines and, more recently, voice mail allow recorded speech to be held till needed.

All these changes result in richer and wider contexts to convey meaning.

The advent of CD ROM technology has advanced the development of multimedia texts still further. CD ROM-based texts can combine print, speech, music, sound effects, pictures, diagrams, animation and video; examples include electronic dictionaries and encyclopedias. The dictionaries have full text searching, allowing the user to find words by searching the meanings or check spelling through successive approximations. More recent versions allow children to locate words through speech input and pictorial clues.

Another change is the use of computer networks and telecommunications to gain access to remote databases. The concept of the virtual library, where books and journals exist in electronic form, stored either in local or remote databases, is beginning to be realised. Australian university libraries are already part of a consortium (Internet) that allows for access to shared collections of electronic texts.

On the horizon, the 'superhighway' and the advent of virtual reality entertainment and learning systems will ensure continuing change in language forms and media. Definitions of literacy will continue to change. Over many centuries societies have moved from oral to written cultures. Today we are moving towards a multimedia electronic world. Literacy will always have communication and information handling at its core, but the commonly identified processes of talking, listening, reading and writing will be extended to include making, viewing and using.

Challenges to schools

All these changes pose significant challenges to education. However, school education has a poor history of successfully meeting the challenge of major shifts in the technologies of communication and information handling (Cuban 1986). Mass schooling has remained embedded in the world of 'words on paper' — literary and factual written texts, books and libraries. The technologies of radio and television have always remained on the periphery, while the telephone has never been seriously considered outside the field of distance education. Even multi-modal printed texts, widespread in the form of young children's picture books, are less commonly made or read in the higher grades, and are seldom deconstructed for their complex meaning and their underlying social and cultural values.

On the surface, as computers become more commonplace in classrooms, it would appear that schooling has taken this particular challenge more seriously. In reality, however, computers have remained on the periphery for the majority of teachers. When they have been moved towards the centre of activity, they have generally been used to generate words on paper. Thus recent research in western countries (e.g. Grunberg & Summers 1992) has found that the most common use of computers in primary schools (and often the only use) has been for word processing — more particularly, for retyping handwritten text to produce 'nice' copy!

Some teachers have moved beyond this stage and have integrated computers into a variety of classroom teaching and learning activities. These teachers have discovered how computers can be used to enhance many aspects of language learning. Examples include:

- the power of small group work at the computer to generate thinking and discussion
- the advantages of using a word processor for the joint construction of text
- the value of text retrieval software in making effective reading strategies explicit
- the potential of desktop publishing software to improve the communicative quality of the published text.

These examples suggest the variety of ways that computers can be used to enhance aspects of talking, listening, reading and writing. The next step is to move beyond existing classroom practices to explore some of the different ways of handling information and communicating that are made possible by computer-related technologies.

Moving beyond print

A major goal of schooling has always been to develop language and literacy skills. But today's children need to become confident and effective users of language in the communication and information media of their world, not of the world in which mass schooling was introduced. Consequently teachers of language need to embrace a wider range of literacies and work with a broader range of texts and media. The notion of 'text' must be redefined to include:

- texts spoken, written, viewed, performed and used
- personal and mass communication
- traditional and electronic texts.

This notion goes a lot further than the use of a computer in the classroom to support existing practices. It challenges teachers to look beyond print, to restore the emphasis on talking and listening (which usually declines over the years of schooling), to include viewing as a distinct mode of communication, and to expand their teaching of English to include multi-modal, mass media and computer-based texts. It also challenges them to deconstruct messages and meanings within images as well as words; to include in, say, a study of humour not only prose and verse, but performances, newspaper cartoons and television shows — even video games; to select videos, audiotapes and electronic texts, as well as books, to support a topic in Science or Society and its Environment. Such changes would reflect the reality of children's lives outside the classroom, besides helping to develop the literacies needed for our changing world.

Some recent curriculum statements have begun to address these issues. The National Statement on English (1993) has defined five modes — speaking, listening, writing, reading and viewing — and the Queensland Department of Education has published a guide entitled *Using Visual Texts in Primary and Secondary English Classrooms*. Regrettably, however, New South Wales has not included viewing in its recent syllabus, nor has Victoria done so for levels 1–3 in the English component of its draft Curriculum and Standards Framework. No education system in Australia has yet tackled the role of computer-based texts in English teaching, although many pay lip service to the role of word processing. Interestingly, though, New Zealand has added visual communication (based on texts from film, television, video and computers) as an integral part of communications skills in its new English syllabus.

The following table provides examples of both traditional and electronic texts that need to be explored in today's classrooms. It includes some processes traditionally linked to drama studies, and inevitably there is some overlap between categories.

Personal Communication	**Speaking/ Listening**	**Writing/ Reading**	**Creating/ Performing**	**Making/Viewing/ Using**
traditional	• conversations • discussions • interviews	• letters • notes • messages • diaries	• role-plays • mimes	• person-to-person explanations or demonstrations using visual aids or apparatus
electronic	• telephone conversations • answering machine messages	• electronic mail (letters, messages, replies) • faxes	• role-plays using electronic networks	• person-to-person use of audiotapes and videotapes
Mass Communication	**Speaking/ Listening**	**Writing/ Reading**	**Creating/ Performing**	**Making/Viewing/ Using**
traditional	• newstimes • lectures • debates • recitals • assembly items	• books • magazines • newspapers • noticeboards • advertisements	• plays • readers theatre • non-verbal performances	• displays • museums and galleries • mass explanations or demonstrations using visual aids or apparatus
electronic	• radio • audiotapes	• bulletin boards • databases • on-line magazines	• adventure games • video games • virtual reality	• TV shows • videos • computer-based visual presentations • computer-based multimedia texts

Texts to be explored in the classroom.

While many teachers are already familiar with the scope of the texts listed, they are not necessarily balancing their priorities and efforts in ways which will enable children to develop understanding and skills with all forms of texts.

Section Three of this book includes a number of classroom stories featuring teachers who are using some of these electronic texts to provide a stimulating environment for children to use and learn language. It should be noted, however, that creating a balance in classrooms need not detract from the rich experiences teachers already provide for children with paper-based texts. Furthermore many of the technical skills required to make props, use a video camera or create a multimedia presentation are part of existing Technology Studies curricula, and the 'design, make, appraise' process which these curricula also include is easily integrated with the creation and publishing of paper-based and electronic multi-modal (or multimedia) products.

How this book can help

While mass media texts and multi-modal printed texts are important ingredients in promoting wider literacy skills, this book concentrates on computer-based texts. It has been organised to assist teachers:

- to get started on using computers in their English teaching
- to develop the use of computers to enhance existing teaching practices
- to explore ways of using computers with a range of electronic texts.

Classroom stories have been used extensively to provide practical examples of successful ideas and teaching strategies for using computers in a range of language learning contexts.

If you are at the 'getting started' stage, go to Chapter 2. There you will meet Maria and Grace, who are about to get started too. You will also find a section called 'Trying it out', setting out a series of steps to help you begin. The final part of the chapter considers a range of issues, such as 'How can I learn more about computers?' and 'How do I develop the children's computing skills?'

If you have already begun to use computers for word processing and so on, go to Section Two. It contains four chapters, all of which include classroom stories, 'Trying it out' sections, and a series of more general questions and answers about the use of computers to enhance talking and listening, reading and writing, and publishing.

If you are already comfortable with designing computer-based learning experiences in a range of language learning contexts, go to Section Three. The three chapters in this section focus on working with electronic texts; the classroom stories introduce ideas for writing, making, viewing, reading and using electronic texts in a wide variety of contexts.

For further reading, viewing or playing

Each chapter ends with a resource list for readers who would like to pursue in greater depth some of the examples and issues raised.

SOCIAL FOCUS

Dyson, S. & McShane, R. 1986, *History of Information Transfer*, Nelson, Melbourne.

Forester, T. 1989, *Computers and the Human Context*, Blackwell, Oxford.

Postman, N. 1993, *Technopoly: The Surrender of Culture to Technology*, Random House, New York. Postman is also the author of *The Disappearance of Childhood* (1984), *Amusing Ourselves to Death* (1985), and *Conscientious Objections: Stirring Up Trouble about Language, Technology and Education* (1988).

Note too that various television documentary series regularly feature technological change and its social impact (e.g. 'Quantum', 'Beyond 2000', and 'Hot Chips').

CURRICULUM FOCUS

English: A Curriculum Profile for Australian Schools 1993, Heinemann, Portsmouth, NH.

Lift Off in the Classroom Series 1993-94, Curriculum Corporation, Melbourne. The series comprises nine packages of video materials and teacher's notes.

O'Brien, A. 1994, 'What about viewing?', *ARA Today: A Quarterly Newsletter from the Australian Reading Association*, no. 3.

Using Visual Texts in Primary and Secondary English Classrooms 1993, Studies Directorate (Humanities), Queensland Department of Education, Brisbane.

Getting Started with Computers

It's only a small step from planning and implementing good quality teaching and learning in English to using computers to enhance your selected outcomes. Making decisions about outcomes, learning experiences, assessment and traditional resources comes first. Considering how to integrate computer use comes second, and it involves checking the availability of hardware and software and organising computer-based learning experiences to enhance the planned outcomes.

The following classroom story concerns two teachers who had been successfully planning and implementing language learning experiences throughout the year but had not as yet included computers as a resource. Their good practice is used as a starting point for describing ways of incorporating computer-based learning to enhance and extend existing practices.

Classroom story

Maria and Grace were team-teaching a class of six- and seven-year-olds. Both were experienced teachers, confidently managing a language program based on the observed needs and interests of the children in their large group. They had agreed that the children needed to develop their ability to work cooperatively and had therefore implemented a range of strategies, including clear guidelines on the roles, rights and expectations of group members, and the development of peer tutoring skills. The children regularly worked in buddy pairs, each partner taking on the role of tutor over a period of time.

A typical morning's language session took place two days after the class had visited a museum — a visit related to the literature-based language unit on dinosaurs they had been working on. The morning began with the whole class gathered on the mat. Greetings and news were exchanged, and then Maria read drafts of several children's individual recounts of their museum visit. After each reading there was a brief discussion of interesting points that had been highlighted, and similarities and differences between the recounts were identified.

Writing focus

Half the group went outside with Grace for some practice with ball skills; the other half — the children who were to act as tutors during buddy time — stayed on the mat with Maria. She had written out the first part of her own recount of the museum excursion and displayed it on an easel.

> Yesterday we went to the museum we thought we were running late so we really hurried along the main street to the railway station we just made it onto the train you should have seen the faces of the people as we noisily piled onto the train when we arrived at Museum station we went up the stairs and through the tunnels to the park where we rested and had a snack

She told the children that she would like some help with punctuating her writing. As a group they read through the recount and began to suggest what punctuation was needed. Some discussion ensued about the kind of punctuation that would best help signpost the meaning. Thoughtful consideration was given to when commas or full stops would be most appropriate and where capital letters should be used. One child suggested that a semi-colon could be used in one sentence, which led to discussion of a new form of punctuation.

After this discussion Maria gave each child a photocopy of the full version of her recount without punctuation. Before the children began the task of punctuating this full text, she used discussion and role play to help them develop a list of points to remember during buddy work:

1. *Make sure both people can see the page – sit beside your buddy.*
2. *Tutors read the words while their buddies track (i.e. follow the words being read).*
3. *Listen for where you need to take a breath.*
4. *Put in commas, full-stops and capital letters.*
5. *Re-read the text to make sure it makes sense.*

When Grace and the other half of the group came back in, the buddy work began. Tutors helped their buddies to read through Maria's recount and together they worked out the punctuation. This phase culminated in a whole group sharing time, where Maria reworked the text as the children took turns to suggest alterations.

Reading focus

Back on the mat as a whole group, Grace encouraged the children to recall what had happened in a dinosaur narrative they had recently read — Robin Klein's *Thing*. Two children from the group were selected to read out loud a synopsis of the story that the class had written as a joint construction and published as a large wall display. In this way Grace introduced the day's shared reading, a sequel to *Thing* entitled *Thingnapped*. The shared reading included lots of opportunities for children to comment on what was happening and predict what they thought might happen next.

Part way into the story Grace stopped reading. She explained to the children that their next task was to create a '*Thingnapped* wordbank' from what they had heard so far. The children worked in groups of four, each group including a scribe and a reporter, and for a while the room was buzzing with excitement. Then, as groups began running out of ideas, the children returned to the mat. One at a time, the reporters came out to share their group's work, reporting their four favourite words from the list compiled. Each wordbank was displayed at the front of the sharing space. Maria and Grace noted the types of temporary spelling the class had used and subsequently planned to focus on them over the next few weeks.

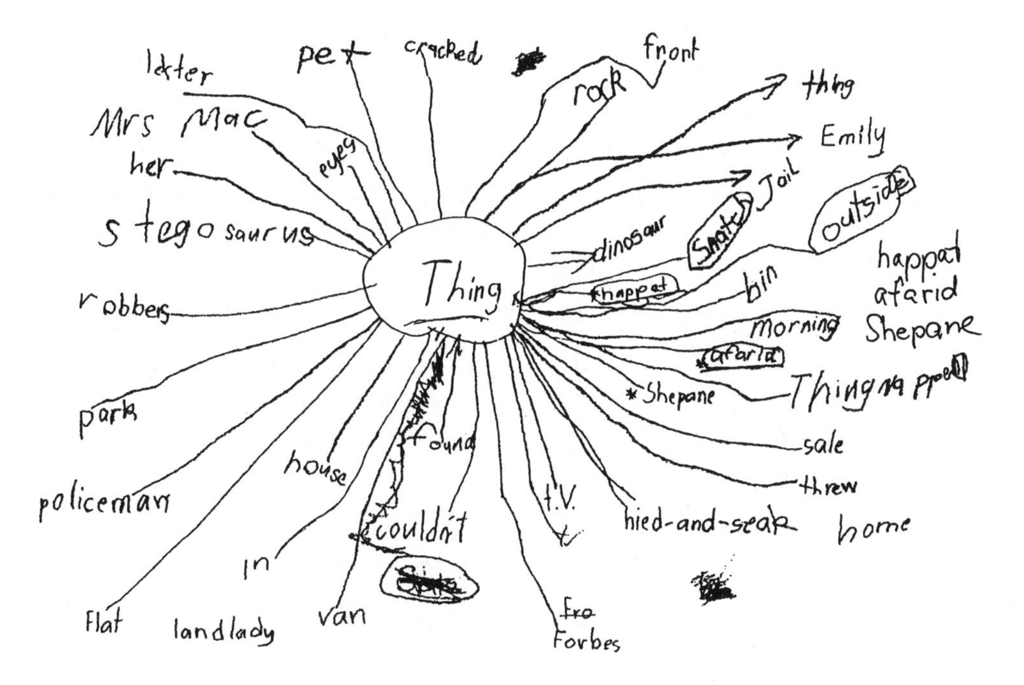

The children produced extensive wordbanks.

Even from this brief description it is clear that this classroom already provided a rich language environment. How could computer-based learning experiences be used to enhance it?

Introducing computers

When we think about introducing computer use into a classroom like this, we have to consider two complementary approaches — namely:

enhancing aspects of some established activities by using computers

extending the nature of the texts with which the children are working.

The following examples are grouped under these two headings. Each example is related to the use of a particular software type, and chapter references have been added to show where you can read about specific ideas in more detail.

Enhancing established activities

§ If the teacher's text is already typed into a word processor without punctuation, buddy partners can work through it on the screen rather than using pen and paper. The public nature of the screen allows both children to see the text easily, which facilitates discussion. Afterwards the punctuated version can be printed out and pairs can share versions, which are easier to read because they are clean. *(Chapter 5)*

§ First drafts of writing can be composed at the computer with a buddy to help. This encourages joint construction and cooperative key finding. *(Chapter 5)*

§ Adventure games can be played by small groups of children. The need to negotiate decisions about the course of the game creates a purposeful oral language environment. Games such as *Dinosaur Discovery* or *Dragon World* would complement the unit of work in Maria and Grace's classroom. *(Chapter 3)*

§ Dinosaur worlds can be created by using a variety of graphics and drawing programs. Images can include stills and/or animation. *(Chapter 3)*

§ Children in small groups can collaboratively reconstruct a familiar text which has been hidden on the computer screen. They can guess or predict words or letters to

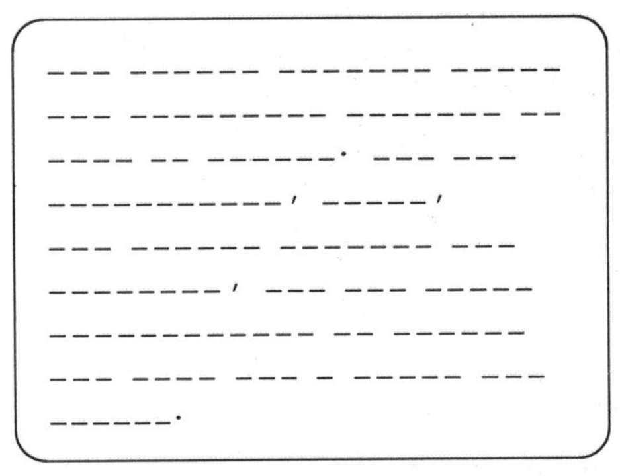

With no contextual clues, reconstruction is very much a matter of guessing, until enough contextual clues are revealed.

One Friday morning Emily had something special to take to school. Her pet s__________, Thing, had helped c______ two burglars, and the Chief Commissioner of P_____ had s___ him a thank you l_____.

With enough contextual clues, reconstruction is based on predicting from meaning.

Two computer screens showing different types of reconstruction task.

rebuild the text (only correct letters and words remain on the screen). Maria and Grace could select sections from *Thing* to give children practice in predicting from meaning. *(Chapter 4)*

§ Children's own written texts about dinosaurs can be published using a word processor and printer. Older students or parent helpers can transcribe edited drafts in the presence of the authors or can scribe for children who dictate their ideas. *(Chapter 5)*

In each example children's language experience is being enriched or enhanced in some way through the use of computers.

Extending the nature of texts

§ Electronic encyclopedias can be searched for different forms of information about dinosaurs: e.g. text, timelines, video, pictures, and possibly voice and sound. *(Chapter 8)*

§ Children's stories about dinosaurs can be published on a word processor disk. Children can browse the collection and read stories from the screen as part of their reading activity. A copy of the stories can be placed on the library computers for other children to read. *(Chapter 7)*

§ A class collection of information about dinosaurs can be made in an electronic form:
- using written text to compile a collection of information reports
- using a record card for each type of dinosaur to make a database
- using written text, images and sounds to create simple multimedia reports about particular dinosaurs. *(Chapters 7 & 8)*

Name:
Where found:
Habitat:
Food:
Stance:
Length:
Weight:
Interesting features:

A record card showing the fields in a dinosaur database.

§ Using electronic mail, children can communicate with another class working on dinosaurs and share information and resources about the dinosaurs they have researched. *(Chapter 9)*

§ Children's factual texts can be published on an electronic bulletin board for other network users to access. *(Chapter 9)*

In these examples children are working with a variety of texts for a variety of purposes — engaged not only in talking, listening, reading and writing, but also in making, viewing and using.

Trying it out

Taking the first step can often seem difficult, particularly if your own computing skills are limited or yet to be developed. The answer is to start simply. Select one type of software, such as a word processor, text retrieval software or an adventure game. This will allow you time to become confident, as well as time to establish some rules and practices about computer use in your classroom. As you gradually add the use of other software types to your repertoire and begin to incorporate a wider range of electronic texts (mass media and computer-based), you will be developing the literacies children need as we move into the 21st century.

Set out below is a series of steps to take you through the planning, implementing and reflecting stages of getting started. Many of the elements mentioned will be exemplified and extended in the following chapters.

Planning

- Identify possible English outcomes, learning experiences and traditional resources.
- Plan for your own learning time; locate experts to provide initial technical support and suggest possible resources. These 'experts' may be colleagues, parents, or children within your own class or other classes.
- Consider using:
  - word processors with some or all of the children during the writing process
  - text retrieval programs drawing on some of the more significant texts included in your reading program
  - adventure games or other problem-solving software to create opportunities for meaningful discussion.
- Check with the librarian or software collection manager about the suitability of the software available.
- Consider how you will use this software to enhance your planned learning outcomes:
  - for joint construction of text?
  - for a focus on cooperative editing?
  - for reconstructing text, using semantic, syntactic and phonetic cues?
  - for a focus on the oral language functions of predicting, hypothesising, justifying and explaining?
- Arrange access to computers for the class, and for individuals and groups within the class. This may involve negotiating with colleagues to have additional computers

for specified periods, access to a computer room, or booked sessions with laptop or other portable computers.

- Consider the organisational issues:
  - location of computers: safety, ease of physical access (including yourself), number of children that can fit comfortably around the screen and keyboard
  - timing of access: timetabling, rotating or free access, set time for tasks or as long as needed
  - grouping: size and composition of groups and appropriate roles within them.

Implementing

- Allocate time and consider strategies for introducing the selected software (e.g. whole class demonstration, peer tutoring).
- Help children to plan for and reflect upon their tasks at the computer.
- Structure time, tasks and roles for computer-related activities as you would for traditional activities.
- Spend time with children working at the computer as well as with other groups in the classroom.
- Display instructions, diagrams and explanations around the computer area to foster children's independence. Encourage them to read these displays, and to consult group members, other classmates or designated computer monitors, before asking you for technical help.
- Monitor learning at the computer as well as in related learning experiences.

Reflecting

- Assess student language learning both at the computer and in other related activities.
- Evaluate the role of the technology. Consider the choice of software, grouping strategies, time allowed at the computer, structure of the task, etc.

Issues to consider when getting started

There is a range of issues to consider whenever we try something new in our classrooms. Sometimes they relate to broader issues of teaching and learning, sometimes to ways of organising for learning. With computers they often relate to the technology itself, as will be evident in the following pages.

How can I learn more about computers?

Learning to use a computer is like learning to drive a car: only regular practice will build up confidence and competence. Likewise it's best to learn with the help of a 'licensed driver'. In any school community or neighbourhood there will be colleagues, parents, local professionals, friends and neighbours who regularly use computers. (A 1994 study by the Australian Bureau of Statistics indicates that 25% of Australian homes have personal computers.) Co-opt one or more of these people to help you learn about computers. If you have no-one beside you, have someone available at the other end of the telephone. Once you have the basic idea, the only way you will develop your own skills is by using the computer regularly.

If you are exploring a piece of software for the first time, try to do so with someone who has used it before. Often novice users who are struggling by themselves fail to recognise the 'learning' potential of a piece of software or overestimate its level of difficulty for children. Adults generally underestimate children's facility with computers.

Computer use can be very frustrating as well as very rewarding, even for experts. Most people using word processors have lost their work at some time or other. In the early stages of computer use, don't be afraid to turn the machine off — after all, you have ultimate control. Right from the start develop some good habits of computer use. Save your work regularly, have copies of important files on at least two different disks and, if you have a hard disk inside your computer, get some advice about making regular backups of your main files. These good habits will not necessarily prevent accidental loss, but they will allow you to retrieve the situation with fewer tears.

As for other forms of support, there are many sources available — both in terms of technical information and of guidelines and advice for using computers with children.

§ Some education systems have computer resource centres or consultants. The centres may offer a range of services, including the loan of hardware and software, provision of inservice courses and consultancy, and production of resource and curriculum materials. Consultants may be able to provide support at the school or classroom level.

§ Some education systems have 'lighthouse' schools or schools designated as centres of excellence in educational computing. Visiting one provides an opportunity to observe good practice and seek advice from other educators.

§ Professional associations which support computer education exist at state and national levels. Also a number of associations which focus on particular curriculum areas have special interest groups devoted to computer use (e.g. the Australian Reading Association).

§ Children in your class or other classes may have had lots of experience with computers and may be glad to act as tutors.

§ Local computer shops or software suppliers may provide consultancy services to help determine hardware and software needs. However, make sure that the support offered extends beyond the date of purchase!

How do I develop children's computing skills?

Children develop computing skills by using computers in a variety of situations for a variety of purposes (sounds familiar?). Just as with language learning, the teaching of specific skills and understanding best occurs within the context of a meaningful task when the learner needs or wants to learn.

Children in your classroom will have a wide range of attitudes and previous experiences with computers, inevitably affecting their perceptions of computer technology and the skills they bring to computer use. If their previous experience has been limited, either by access or type of software, then what you do in your classroom must compensate for these limitations. You need to ensure that all children have access to appropriate technology and a variety of experiences, and that learning is maximised through supportive classroom management and adult interaction.

When you are planning to introduce computers, there are a number of things you should do.

- Find out whether or not families have a computer at home. Are the children allowed to use it? If so, how do they use it, how often and for how long? Is it only a game-playing machine or can it be used for word processing?
- Be prepared to offer separate, additional experiences, at least initially, to meet the needs of children with no previous computer experience. Provide explicit teaching of computer-related vocabulary and concepts, and publish jointly constructed rules, advice and instructions, so that all children can become independent computer users.
- Value the expertise that some children will bring to your classroom. Help them to develop tutoring skills so that they don't try to take over when they are assisting others.
- Plan a variety of experiences using different types of software to show children that computers can be more than games machines.
- Become familiar with the world of electronic games that children play outside school. Engage them in conversation about games, plots and action in the same way as you would discuss books or their own writing. Respond to key issues they may mention: for example, violence, gender roles or the fantasy/reality dichotomy.
- Develop a roster system or some means of allocating turns at the computer to ensure that all children have a similar share of time. Monitor situations where activities are self-selected to ensure that all children are able to gain access at some stage.
- Keep an eye on group dynamics when children are working together at the computer. It's often better to combine children of equal assertiveness. Alternatively each child can be given a particular role, determined by the software, and later roles can be swapped. Possible roles include keyboarding or mouse control, note-taking, observing or tutoring. Give all children opportunities to take a leadership role.

➤ Select software that appeals to boys and girls (in terms of both content and process) but does not present gender stereotypes. Introduce a variety of applications throughout the year so that boys and girls will experience using a computer for a variety of purposes. All children will be disadvantaged if only one type of software is continually used.

How do I find out about and select software for use?

FINDING OUT ABOUT WHAT IS AVAILABLE

§ Most schools have a computer coordinator or librarian responsible for the school software collection. These colleagues are an invaluable resource when you need to know about the software currently held by the school.

§ Software reviews appear regularly in a variety of publications. Many professional association newsletters, magazines and journals carry reviews. The school librarian is probably the best person to approach about where to find software reviews.

§ Major software suppliers usually publish catalogues which are available free of charge. They provide a good starting point when you are looking for software, but you should never make a purchase based solely on information supplied in a catalogue. Catalogues are designed to sell something and so rarely provide unbiased reviews.

SELECTING SOFTWARE FOR USE

§ Assessing the learning potential of a piece of software must take the highest priority. If it doesn't suit the children for whom you are planning, there's no point in going any further! Software should be consistent with your philosophy of children's language learning and should have the potential to cater for a wide range of individual needs, strengths and interests.

§ You need to be able to easily identify what learning outcomes you will be able to realise by using a particular piece of software. You must also balance the time needed to learn and use it against the expected outcomes. Although some software is complex or time-consuming to use, it may be the very stuff to create an exciting language learning environment. Word processors, for example, require keyboard familiarity and a developing knowledge of disk handling, saving and loading files, and using printers. By contrast, adventure games are very easy to use but time-consuming to play. These 'costs' need to be outweighed by the benefits of use.

§ The content of the software should be evaluated by the same criteria that you would apply to any classroom resource, including children's literature or factual texts. Content needs to be developmentally appropriate, cater for a range of skills and understandings, and be free of gender and racial stereotypes.

§ You should check what support is available for using the software (including local 'experts'). Many software packages come with an accompanying booklet or on-screen support; such instructions should describe clearly how the software works and how to operate specific features within the program.

§ While user-friendliness is a desirable feature and commonly found with recently developed software, adults are more inclined to find 'less friendly' software off-putting than children are. If the software appears difficult to use, track down someone who has used it in a classroom and seek advice. If the learning potential warrants it, take the time to learn to use it well, identify possible trouble spots and demonstrate appropriate strategies to the children.

§ You should always check what hardware features are required to operate the software — viz:
  - the brand and model of computer needed
  - the amount of memory (RAM) needed and whether or not a hard drive or CD ROM drive is essential
  - whether or not a printer is required
  - whether any other peripheral devices are essential or desirable (for example, some software requires a mouse; other programs work most effectively if a sound card has been installed in the computer).

How do I organise access to computers?

Schools vary in the way they set up their computers. Possibilities include:

- one computer in each classroom
- one computer shared between several classrooms
- two or more computers in each classroom
- all the school's computers in one classroom (often known as the computer room)
- all the computers in the library
- some computers in a computer room, with others available for booking out to individual classes
- one computer in each classroom, with a number of laptop computers available for booking out to individual classes
- combinations of the above.

Each of these set-ups allows for different types of access, some of which may be particularly suitable for certain applications. No one approach is inherently better than another, though obviously access to more computers offers a wider range of choice.

One of the most desirable features in a school's computer policy is the sort of flexibility that allows teachers to organise access to suit their purposes. After all, different uses have different time demands, and you have to take account of them in your planning. Further, if you are sharing a computer room with classes of children ranging between five and twelve years, issues of ergonomics and safety will also need attention. For example, when younger children are using older children's furniture, footstools that can be pushed out of the way when not required are a simple solution.

As new computers are purchased, the use of old and new machines should be integrated. Older computers which do not support images and sound are still quite valuable: for instance, a word processor can be used for joint construction of text and reading stories from the screen. Children will readily move from one brand or model of computer to another, even within their own classroom.

When computer access is very limited, decisions about priority use must be carefully considered. Research suggests that children with special needs benefit greatly from using computers (Hawkridge & Vincent 1992). This includes children with learning difficulties, those with poor motor skills (and illegible handwriting), and those with language disorders. Decisions based on special needs are more defensible than giving priority to older children in the school or early finishers in the classroom.

How do I go about assessing children's learning at the computer?

The How and What of assessment should stem directly from your language outcomes, which you will have selected from the English curriculum statements used by your system or school. The When and Where can be extended to include children's interactions with and around computers, and work they have produced using computers. You also need to encourage self-assessment of learning in computer contexts, just as you do with other language experiences.

In addition, *Technology: A Curriculum Profile for Australian Schools* (1994) has profiles and pointers for the information technology strand that can be applied to the whole range of computer-based learning experiences you are providing. Most state curricula or syllabuses also include information technology strands in one or other of their key learning areas. These guidelines can be used to shape outcomes and the 'design, make and evaluate' process that might come into play when children are using computer-based tools to create presentations such as posters, screen-based slide shows or multimedia products.

Further opportunities for assessing children's language learning include:

- observing children working at the computer, and during their planning sessions beforehand and their reflection sessions afterwards
- noting children's contributions to Players Circles (see Chapter 3)
- conferencing with individual children or small groups while they are using the computer, or before or after computer use
- collecting printouts or samples of children's computer-related work (e.g. interpretations of graphs produced on the computer).

Some record of the processes children have used while working at the computer may be available, depending on the software. For example, if children are using a word processing program, it's possible to save progressive drafts of their writing. Some talking book software records words that children select to hear, while some problem-solving or tutorial programs allow you to access a record of the decision-making processes that individual children have used.

For further reading, viewing or playing

Books

Fatouros, C., Downes, T. & Blackwell, S. 1994, *In Control: Young Children Learning with Computers*, Social Science Press, Wentworth Falls, NSW.

Scrimshaw, P. (ed.) 1994, *Language, Classrooms and Computers*, Routledge, New York.

Curriculum guidelines

Technology: A Curriculum Profile for Australian Schools 1994, Curriculum Corporation, Melbourne.

Note too that in the past ten years most state and territory educations systems have published a range of curriculum statements and support documents on the use of computers in primary schools. More recently these statements have been superseded by the inclusion of computer use in the information technology strands of most Technology Studies documents. Even so, the earlier documents are useful reading for those getting started. A number of curriculum statements from other key learning areas, such as English or Mathematics, may also contain references to computer use.

Videos

Hands On: The Computing Kit 1987, Disadvantaged Schools Program, Metropolitan East Region, Sydney. The kit contains two videocassettes and three teacher support books.

SECTION TWO

Talking and Listening

Over the last decade, researchers have consistently found that small groups using a computer often generate much more oral language, of higher quality, than groups involved in more traditional learning experiences. In fact the computer area has been described as a social centre (Beaty & Tucker 1987).

However, providing opportunities for children to interact is not in itself a guarantee that they will learn what you want them to learn. You have to take an active role in managing the learning environment to ensure the success of the experiences you have planned. You can support children's learning in the way that you explain, organise and relate a task to other learning experiences. For example, while children are working with computers, your choice of software and methods of grouping can both help to support their learning (Mercer 1994).

Open-ended software is generally most effective in promoting talking and listening for a variety of purposes. 'Open-ended' here refers to programs that allow children to control the direction and pace of their interaction, and where there are no right or wrong answers. Examples include drawing and painting programs, some adventure games, word processors, music-making programs and other graphic construction or text creation programs. These types of software:

- allow users to negotiate their own goals (e.g. a drawing program allows them to decide what they want to create; a word processing program allows them to decide what they want to write)
- provide a variety of ways of achieving goals (e.g. children need to decide how to go about creating a particular drawing or which path to take through an adventure).

In this chapter we will look at two teachers using different software programs and grouping methods, with the common aim of developing a range of talking and listening skills.

Cooperative problem solving with children beginning school

The following classroom story tells how the teacher, Anna, created an effective learning environment by selecting an open-ended software program and having children use it in friendship pairs. The drawing program she selected allowed the children to decide for themselves what they wanted to create and how long they wanted to spend creating it. Within this context she interacted with the children to develop their skills in cooperative problem solving.

Classroom story

All but two of the children in Anna's class were from language backgrounds other than English. Many were from Vietnamese and Cantonese language backgrounds, but there were also children from Serbian, Croatian, Cambodian and Italian backgrounds. Naturally language was always a major focus and, as well as promoting the use of English, Anna encouraged children to use their first language. Although this often occurred naturally amongst groups with the same first language, she was able to promote it further by inviting other adults (support teachers and family members) to work with children in their first language.

When setting up learning experiences for younger children, Anna's usual policy was to make available enough of a particular resource for several children to participate at one time, each having his or her individual piece of play-dough, jigsaw puzzle or whatever it might be. However, there was only one computer in the classroom, which meant that the children needed to develop their skills in sharing and cooperating.

A computer learning centre had been an integral part of the classroom since the beginning of the year. It was usually set up with two or three chairs and children were free to have a turn whenever they wanted, provided there was a spare chair. Anna usually placed a timer near the computer so that children could negotiate turn-taking independently.

One of Anna's main goals in setting up the computer centre had been to stimulate oral language. However, close observation of children around the computer showed her that the established arrangement did not always lead to effective interactions. The child using the mouse or the keyboard was often totally absorbed in what was happening on the screen, while the other child or children sat silently waiting for a

Using a timer allowed the children to negotiate turn-taking independently.

turn. Promoting greater use of oral language (and therefore learning from each other) required a new grouping strategy.

Working collaboratively

Anna had noticed that the most effective interactions around the computer generally occurred when two friends were working together. Sometimes a group of three was also effective, depending on the children involved, but for most of the children pairs tended to work more amicably. With this in mind, Anna asked the children to choose a friend who would be their 'computer partner'. Whenever children went to the computer, they went with their computer partner. Names and photos of the pairs were displayed on a chart nearby for ready reference by children, staff and parents.

The children's interactions at the computer also varied according to the type of software being used, with the most productive talk occurring when they were using open-ended software that allowed them to decide their own goal and determine their own pace. The following discussion had been recorded earlier between three children using *Kid Pix 2*, a draw/paint program specifically designed for young children:

KENNY: *(to Melissa, who is carefully arranging stamps in a circular pattern on the screen)* What are you making? Circles?

MELISSA: No.

KENNY: No . . . *(labelling stamps Melissa has used)* Flowers, trees and ties.

MELISSA: Bows. *(She points to the bow stamp)*
KENNY: They're not bows, ties. Ties, aren't they, Tam?
MELISSA: They're bows.
KENNY: Ties!
TAM: Tie bows. They're tie bows.
KENNY: Yeah. Tie bows.
TAM: That's fair, OK? That's fair.

On another occasion Anna observed the children using a more structured learning game. The children loved this piece of software as it was colourful and animated and the on-screen characters actually 'talked' to them, providing directions, prompts and feedback. It had one particular disadvantage, however: the interaction at the computer was often focused between the child using the mouse and the on-screen characters. Children would frequently answer the characters or ask them questions, and in doing so would totally ignore their computer partner.

Since the goal was to promote talking and listening, Anna decided to continue using *Kid Pix 2*. But the children still needed some adult help initially to develop their skills in working together. Anna began by working closely with each pair whilst the remainder of the children were engaged in experiences they could complete independently. Her intention was not only to assist the children in using the software, but also to help them develop skills in cooperative problem solving (i.e. what to make, how to begin, what drawing tool to select, what to do when things didn't go as expected, how to negotiate turns with their partner, etc.). The goal was for the children to collaborate in making a picture together rather than each working on an individual creation. The following interaction occurred between two children after several sessions with Anna's assistance:

Ming is using the mouse. His computer partner, Kim, is directing him and using the keyboard to enlarge the stamps that Ming adds to their picture . . .

KIM: Get a colour.
MING: Dark blue?
KIM: If you want.
MING: *(as he positions the cursor on the colour palette)* That one?
KIM: Yeah. *(She reaches across to help with the mouse)*
Now! Pour the colour on!
MING: *(referring to the screen, now filled with a dark blue colour)* Now . . . what do you want in the deep blue sea?
KIM: Fishes.
MING: OK. Now what do I press?
KIM: *(to the teacher)* We want the fishes . . .
TEACHER: You need the stamps. Do you remember how to get the stamps?
MING: Oh yeah!
KIM: *(pointing to the stamp tool)* There it is.

	(Ming selects the stamp tool and they scroll through the stamps to find some fish)
TEACHER:	Now, you'll need to decide what size you want them.
KIM:	Big! *(She searches the keyboard for the appropriate key)*
MING:	Press!
	(Kim presses the key)
MING:	Big shark!!!
	(Both laugh)

Trying it out

- Decide on your language focus and select software and grouping methods accordingly. For example, if you want to develop talking and listening skills, consider whether you want to encourage children to use English or their first language, or to learn new vocabulary. The learning goal will determine the most suitable method of grouping and will also have implications for the type of software used.
- Select software to match your learning goal. Open-ended software is most effective if the goal is to promote problem solving and negotiation.
- Experiment with different grouping strategies to maximise the amount and type of talk. We've seen how Anna found that the children in her class interacted most effectively when they worked in friendship pairs. This method of grouping led to more sharing, turn-taking and more talk in general. She also found that small language-based groups led by a support teacher or parent were the most effective way of encouraging children to use their first language.
- Help children to become independent users of the software. Then you can concentrate on developing their skills in solving problems together. For example, charts and posters with instructions about how to load a program or how to print will help to foster their independence; a timer will allow them to monitor their own turn-taking. You should also give them time to practise and develop their confidence in using the software.
- Plan your own role to foster talking and listening. The following sequence of skills (Elliott 1994) is a useful guide.

  Step 1 – negotiating shared goals. Identifying and clarifying a goal is the essential first step if children are to develop a shared focus. Suggest a broad goal to begin with, and then encourage children to refine it to suit their own interests. For example, if you suggest that they use the drawing tools to make a picture, they need to discuss and agree what their picture should be like. You need to make sure that each child is actively involved and contributing to the process.

  Step 2 – cooperatively planning actions to achieve the goal. Once children have decided what they want to achieve, they need help to move towards their goal in small steps. This help may take the form of guiding instructions or questions: e.g. *Let's decide what we're going to do. What do we need to do first? Now what should we do next?* Again, each child should be encouraged to contribute to the discussion and planning; leaving all decisions to one person (child or teacher) defeats the purpose. You can give encouragement by:

- providing meaningful feedback on choices made or actions taken (feedback should give genuine information about what a child has done well: e.g. *It was a good idea to try out all those options and find out what they could do. Now you'll know which one to use*)
- emphasising that small and manageable steps will ensure success, and assisting children to sequence these smaller steps
- identifying and providing positive feedback on ideas as well as solutions
- building on children's previous knowledge and understandings through all stages.

Step 3 – evaluating actions. Children need help to reflect on their actions and become more aware of successful and unsuccessful strategies. You can help by providing meaningful feedback and questioning their choices: e.g. *Why did you choose that tool? Could you have used something else? Did that do what you wanted? Do you remember what you used last time? What might happen if . . . ?*

Adventure games with eleven- and twelve-year-olds

The term 'adventure game software' refers to story-based programs that give the user some control over the plot. Usually the software simulates an imaginary world which is described in words or pictures, and quite often the user takes the role of hero. There's usually a quest or mission to be accomplished and a series of hazards and obstacles to overcome along the way. Since adventure game software often involves a great deal of problem solving and decision making, it lends itself to small group work. Small groups provide an excellent context for promoting a range of different types of oral language, such as arguing, conjecturing, justifying, theorising, hypothesising and explaining.

Classroom story

Tom noticed that the children in his class needed to develop further skills in talking and listening for a variety of purposes and a variety of audiences. Convinced that these skills were essential for all learning across the curriculum, he was concerned that they were often neglected in upper primary grades, where reading and writing took precedence. In particular, he wanted to give the children opportunities to discuss ideas and issues in a small group context and to be involved in presenting information and ideas to a larger audience (the whole class). This meant that they needed to practise:

- listening and responding appropriately to others
- using questions effectively
- selecting and sequencing information for spoken presentations.

All the children in the class were experienced computer users, and Tom had already been doing a lot of work to develop their skills in cooperative learning. Most of them were progressing well, though there were a few exceptions. Two children in particular did not function well in groups, preferring to work on their own. As a result, whatever group they worked in tended to split the work between the members rather than working together. Another child had problems cooperating and the other members of his group always complained about his behaviour.

A unit of work

With these concerns in mind, Tom designed an integrated unit of work that provided plenty of opportunities for cooperative talking and listening. The focus question was, 'How can people live in harmony with their environment?' Well aware of the potential of computer-based learning experiences to promote discussion, Tom selected an adventure game called *Flowers of Crystal* as a basis for much of the work. The goal of this game was to save the imaginary world of Crystal from a variety of evil forces — both human and environmental. Included in the software package was an audiotape which told the story of the Flowers of Crystal, providing a more meaningful context for the children's use of the game.

Tom also planned other talking and listening activities away from the computer, as well as tasks that included reading and writing different text types for a variety of purposes. The class focus on 'The Environment' provided a context for all these activities, and reading, writing, talking and listening were often interwoven.

In addition, Tom planned a variety of learning experiences in a range of other curriculum areas — for example:

- research on specific environmental issues, such as damage to the ozone layer and destruction of the world's rainforests
- experiments to determine the ideal conditions for the growth of different types of plants
- problem-solving activities related to the types of mathematical problems encountered in the software (e.g. using map grids and multiplication tables)
- visual arts activities aimed at creating an imaginary world in the classroom and costumes and masks for role-plays.

Every day Tom devoted the morning session to the unit. The children worked in groups of five, with a different group having a turn at the computer each day. The

TALKING
- Discussing issues related to the story
- Small group discussion and decision making while playing the game
- Sharing game-playing strategies with others during Players Circles
- Role-playing characters from the story
- Presenting role-plays to an audience
- Interviewing characters as part of the role-plays
- Debating environmental issues

LISTENING
- Listening to the story on audiotape
- Listening to other people's opinions/arguments (both at and away from the computer) and responding appropriately
- Listening to other children's game-playing strategies during Players Circles
- Listening to shared readings of literature

HOW CAN PEOPLE LIVE IN HARMONY WITH THEIR ENVIRONMENT?

READING
- Reading the story from the booklet included in the software package
- Reading clues from the computer screen
- Sharing literature with a conservation theme
- Researching books about the environment
- Reading newspaper articles

WRITING
- Writing logs of each computer session
- Preparing interview questions for role-plays
- Writing book reports and character studies
- Recording progress of the plant experiments
- Writing letters to politicians about environmental issues

An overview of Tom's English program.

other groups were engaged in related activities away from the computer, such as writing and illustrating their adventure game logs, checking and documenting the progress of their experiments, or discussing and planning strategies for their next turn at the computer.

At the computer

When working at the computer, children were required to allocate a specific role to each group member. These roles were rotated each session so that all children gained a variety of perspectives and had opportunities to talk and listen for a variety of purposes. The roles were:

reader: to read the screen clues aloud to the rest of the group

decision-maker: to resolve group discussion about what equipment to take and what choices to make

keyboarder: to key in the group's responses

A great deal of environmental print was generated by small group discussions at the computer.

recorder: to note down details of each session (to be written up later as a log)

resource person: to have available paper and pencils, as well as any aids developed from previous sessions (e.g. maps showing the position of 'Zap gates' and other hazards encountered in the game).

Assigning specific roles at the computer was particularly beneficial for the children in Tom's class who found cooperative work difficult. As each person in the group had a specific task to do, it was impossible for one group member to complete the activity independently.

There was always a lively discussion at the computer as children read clues, argued about decisions, recalled previous sessions and delighted in their current progress. These discussions were continued away from the computer as children conferenced together to write up their log.

Another regular feature of Tom's classroom was the Players Circle. This was a whole class discussion in which children were encouraged to identify and share the successful strategies that their group had used at the computer. It also provided Tom with a further means of evaluating the children's progress.

Trying it out

- Select software that presents sustained challenges rather than a loose collection of puzzles and tasks. Challenges large enough to be tackled over several sessions at the computer create a more fruitful context for speculating, hypothesising and justifying decisions.

- Select an adventure game related to literature-based work in English or a unit in Science or Society and its Environment. The software should be an additional resource rather than the reason for planning the unit.
- Identify aspects of the adventure game that relate to other key learning areas. For example, the threatened extinction of the Crystal Flower in the adventure game Tom had selected sparked experiments with the conditions needed for seed germination and plant growth, which developed the children's understandings in Science.
- Consider ways of creating meaningful opportunities for talking, listening, reading and writing. At the computer children need to read the clues from the screen and debate their choices. By interpreting the on-screen responses, they can hypothesise about the outcome of future choices. There should also be opportunities for them to reflect on and talk over each computer session as a follow-up activity. Writing up a log of the choices made and the information gathered provides a resource for future sessions.
- Plan a range of small group activities to allow effective use of one computer in the classroom. While one group is using the computer, the other groups can be involved in related experiences.
- Try to spend time interacting with the group at the computer as well as with other groups. However, when that's not possible, spend some time before and after the session assisting with the planning and evaluation of the group's interactions. This will help to maximise the talk that goes on around the computer.
- Provide frequent opportunities for children to develop skills in cooperative group work. For example, Tom started the children working in pairs and threes before he moved them to groups of five.
- Involve children in developing rules for group work both at the computer and away from it. Giving children some ownership of the rules usually means that they will ensure the rules are followed.
- Assign roles during group work and ensure that all children experience a variety of roles over a period of time. This provides opportunities for children to practise talking and listening in different contexts and from different perspectives.
- Set aside time for Players Circles. They provide a meaningful context for talking and listening, encouraging children to articulate the strategies they have been using to work through the adventure game. The sharing of successful strategies is beneficial to all children.
- Help children to evaluate their own performance. Suggest possible questions: e.g. *What strategies did we use that were successful/unsuccessful? Why did these succeed/not succeed? What other strategies could we use?*

Issues to consider when planning to enhance talking and listening

What features of a software program are most effective in promoting talking and listening?

While we've seen that open-ended software can be very effective in promoting cooperative problem solving, some other types of software may actually inhibit talk. For example, fast and furious arcade-style games can become very competitive — even addictive — with the child using the mouse or keyboard focusing on improving his or her score and paying little attention to anything but the computer. Even structured puzzles or learning games, particularly those with on-screen characters that 'talk' to the user, focus the relationship between the child and the screen. While these types of software may be useful for achieving other learning goals, they do not maximise oral interaction.

However, adventure games can provide a motivating context for cooperative group work and consequently much discussion. Features to look for when selecting adventure game software include:

- a strong sense of narrative, including a well-described setting, a range of characters, a clearly stated objective and plot development throughout the adventure (these features provide a basis for decision making and allow children to identify and discuss reasons for their choices as they work their way through the adventure)
- concise on-screen text and easy-to-follow instructions (if the instructions include some graphic cues to cater for developing readers or children from language backgrounds other than English, all can follow the game and take part in decision making and related discussion)
- the facility to save the game at any stage (a feature which allows children not only to resume the adventure at a later stage if they run out of time, but also to save their progress at critical stages and avoid having to start again from the beginning).

This strategy of saving at critical points, which may need to be explicitly taught, is a way of helping children to deal constructively with occasions when the group is having problems reaching a consensus. The game can be saved before a controversial decision is tried out, and if the decision proves to be the wrong one, the game can be resumed from the version saved on disk and an alternative tried.

What types of talk can be promoted by sharing a computer?

Open-ended software with no predetermined responses and no time limits is ideal for promoting cooperative problem solving. Since it allows children to set their own goals, decide how they will work towards them and assess their progress from time to time, it encourages lots of talk and negotiation at each stage. In addition, draw/paint and other graphic construction software can foster the use of imaginative language as children create their own pictures and develop fantasies around them. As always, however, the grouping method is important, with children being more likely to engage in this type of language use if they are working in a supportive friendship group.

Adventure games, simulations and other problem-solving programs provide many opportunities for prediction and for formulating and testing hypotheses. Children have to argue for and justify their decisions and then form new hypotheses based on the consequences of those decisions. However, as noted above with the 'save' option, it is important that the software allows ideas to be tested and decisions to be changed once children have seen the consequences. Many programs (such as draw/paint programs and word processors) have an 'undo' option that allows the last action to be reversed; like the 'save' option, this may need to be explicitly taught.

What issues need to be considered when organising groups to work at the computer?

Small groups have long been recognised as effective learning contexts for people of all ages. Small group interaction has also been recognised as a supportive context for second language learners (Gibbons 1991). However, effective group work doesn't just happen; children need opportunities to learn how to work as members of a group. Computer-based experiences provide an environment in which they can do so as they develop their skills in solving problems cooperatively. Nevertheless, when the learning goal is to promote talking and listening, several issues need to be considered.

Firstly, the size of groups is important. Pairs are often most effective with younger children; if they are gathered around the computer in larger groups, some tend to be left out of the conversation. With older children and larger groups, assigning group roles is often the best way of ensuring maximum interaction.

The composition of the group and the way it works are also important. A collaborative approach (rather than a turn-taking one) means that children talk more and are more likely to work cooperatively towards a shared goal, instead of sitting as spectators waiting for a turn. Groups formed on a friendship or interest basis are likely to lead to closer collaboration. In some cases same gender groups may be more conducive to talking and listening, as some children, particularly older ones, are inclined to feel more at ease with their own sex.

The time groups are given to work at the computer may also affect the amount of talk. For example, if a time limit is placed on each group, children feel pressured and will often focus more attention on the screen, usually at the expense of interaction with each other. Allowing them to stay at the computer until they have completed a set task relieves the pressure and gives more room for discussion.

Planning for small group or whole class discussions away from the computer may also help to increase the amount of talk that goes on at the computer. One example of this we've already seen is Tom gathering his whole class together for Players Circles. Another possibility is that a member of each computer group joins the Players Circle to share successful strategies and then reports back to the group.

How can computers be used to enhance talking and listening skills for second language learners?

Computer-based learning experiences allow children to hear many different language models. They hear the teacher's language when he or she demonstrates the use of the software; they hear the language of their peers interacting at the computer when they are 'just watching'; they use language themselves when they are negotiating choices and when they are preparing for and reflecting upon computing tasks. Nevertheless there are a few particular points to bear in mind when you are planning to use a computer with children from diverse language backgrounds.

- The planned experience needs to be a meaningful one. The software selected should therefore be related to the children's other classroom experiences, so that they already have a developing vocabulary, an established repertoire of language structures and a growing understanding of the content. The software should also provide models of natural, predictable language and plenty of opportunities for the children to interact.
- One concern with using drill and practice programs is that they usually consist of activities with no context and so are unlikely to create the meaningful small group learning situations that second language learners need. In addition, many of these types of program involve working within a set time frame, which reduces opportunities for interaction between children.
- There may be opportunities within the context of a computer-based learning experience to promote children's use of their first language. Grouping young children by language background may mean that this occurs spontaneously.

For further reading, viewing or playing

Books and articles

Bell, S. 1986, 'Children, language and computers', *Classroom Computing*, vol. 8, no.1, pp.15-22.

Fisher, E. 1993, 'The teacher's role', in P. Scrimshaw (ed.), *Language, Classrooms and Computers*, Routledge, New York.

Mercer, N. 1994, 'The quality of talk in children's joint activity at the computer', *Journal of Computer-Assisted Learning*, vol. 10, no 1, pp.24-32.

Videos

Talking Point 1984, MEP, England. This British-made classroom video explores the use of computers in language learning, particularly with regard to talking and listening.

Videos

Hands On: The Computing Kit 1987, Disadvantaged Schools Program, Metropolitan East Region, Sydney. The kit contains two videocassettes and three teacher support books.

Software

ADVENTURE GAMES

Carmen Sandiego (DOS, Macintosh, Windows, Macintosh/Windows CD ROM).
Dinosaur Discovery (Macintosh & MPC CD ROM).
Gizmos & Gadgets (Macintosh, Windows, Macintosh/Windows CD ROM).
Go West! CD (Macintosh CD ROM/Windows CD ROM).
Magic School Bus (Macintosh/Windows CD ROM).
Sim City 2000 (DOS, Macintosh, Windows, Macintosh/Windows CD ROM)
The Amazon Trail (DOS, Macintosh, Windows, Macintosh/Windows CD ROM).
The Oregon Trail (Apple, DOS, Macintosh, Windows, Macintosh/Windows CD ROM).

DRAW/PAINT PROGRAMS

Easy Color Paint (Macintosh).
Flying Colors (Macintosh, Windows, Macintosh/Windows CD ROM).
Kid Pix 2 (DOS, Macintosh, Windows).

GRAPHIC CONSTRUCTION

Monsters and Make Believe Plus (Apple II, DOS, Macintosh).
Transportation Transformation (Apple II, DOS).

Reading

There are many opportunities for enhancing reading while children are working at the computer. For example, using adventure games (as in Chapter 3) or word processing software (as in Chapter 5) involves reading for a variety of purposes. Children may be reading the screen for instructions on how to use the program or to discover another clue as they work through an adventure; they may be re-reading their own writing to edit it or reading texts that other children have published.

The general principles for planning any literature-based reading activities should also apply to the planning of computer-based activities designed to enhance reading ability. Most importantly, the starting point for all planned experiences should be the selected text, the children's strengths, needs and interests, and the teacher's purposes (Nicoll & Roberts 1993). It's easy to overlook this principle as we become intrigued with the enticing features of the hardware and the latest developments in software. However, if a piece of software is not consistent with your own philosophy of children's learning, then you should not use it.

Software programs should be sufficiently flexible to allow you to adapt them to support the learning you are planning. Beware of using programs that do not allow a variety of possible responses or pathways. Colourful screen displays and clever animation are no indication of the learning potential inherent in software programs. Rather, you should judge them by the same criteria as you judge any other resource that you are planning to incorporate in your classroom program.

The specific activities described in this chapter demonstrate how software may either be tailored to suit the strengths, needs and interests of the children (as with the text completion program), or may be so open-ended that children can respond at their own level (as with designing the concept keyboard overlays). In both cases, the software selected provides a framework which either teacher or children can adapt to their particular needs, and the screen display is designed to be purposeful rather than visually engaging.

Text reconstruction as a strategy for developing readers

Text reconstruction software allows the teacher to type in a passage of text and then hide certain parts, leaving only selected words, letters or punctuation marks visible. The goal for children is to reconstruct the text through a combination of prediction and guesswork. Text reconstruction at the computer is similar to the widespread use of cloze, although there are some important differences which are summarised in the table below.

CLOZE ACTIVITIES	TEXT RECONSTRUCTION PROGRAMS
Different deletion patterns can be used, depending on the goal of the activity and the reading level of the children participating.	Various levels of clues can be provided to match learning goals and the needs and strengths of the children participating.
The same amount of space is left for each missing word, as the aim is to substitute an appropriate word.	A blank space is indicated for each missing letter of each word, as the aim is to match the original text.
Oral cloze can be used with small groups or the whole class; written (pencil and paper) cloze can be completed by individuals or small groups.	The focus is on written language, and ideally children should work in small groups, with one child keying in the group's suggestions. All group members can see the consequences of their suggestions displayed on the screen.
Anything written on paper becomes a 'permanent' record of children's attempts, and while this has advantages for assessment, it can make children reluctant to experiment.	The computer allows children to try out predictions and gain immediate feed-back; if the attempt is incorrect, the typing disappears from the screen, leaving a clean text to work on.
Children can fill gaps with any word that makes sense in the context. A critical understanding to be developed is that meaning is more important than getting each word 'right' (Parker & Unsworth 1986).	Only the exact word is accepted; if a different word is entered, it will disappear from the screen. The aim is text matching, which should be supported by the presence of appropriate contextual clues or the use of familiar passages.

What appears on the initial screen display of a text reconstruction program is controlled by the teacher. Several sample screens are included in the following classroom story, and here are some other possibilities:

- When children have demonstrated difficulty in predicting structure words (e.g. conjunctions, pronouns, prepositions) during oral reading, a passage of text can be prepared with only structure words removed.

- When the goal is to increase children's vocabulary, unfamiliar words can be removed, perhaps leaving initial sounds or other phonetic clues; children have to predict what the words might be from the context provided by the rest of the passage.
- When the goal is to develop readers' understanding of the organisation of ideas in a text, a screen can be prepared to display a few key words from a familiar passage, with markers showing the number of words and the number of letters in each word for the remainder of the text. This is similar to macro-cloze (Parker & Unsworth 1986).

With this type of software, children use a variety of reading and problem-solving strategies: for example, trying to identify an overall theme or context, trying to match meaningful groups of letters (morphemes) with their own knowledge of morphemes, and predicting words from their position in the text and relationship to other nearby words. These strategies are the same as those used by effective readers.

Classroom story

The children in Jemima's class were seven- and eight-year-olds, ranging from developing readers to independent readers. Their morning always began with a two-hour language session, during which they alternated between working as a whole class and working in small groups, friendship pairs or individually. One of the small group activities each morning was usually computer-based. Jemima had permanent access to one computer and at times she negotiated with colleagues to have the use of several computers simultaneously.

This term the class had been focusing on the Aboriginal tradition of Dreaming stories. Jemima wanted to develop the children's awareness of their spiritual significance for Aboriginal people. Each week she planned a variety of activities related to one particular story. The children had already read quite a number of the stories and were beginning to recognise their distinguishing features.

One morning Jemima started with a whole class session, encouraging the children to consider what they could recall about how Dreaming stories begin. She asked them to predict whether or not all stories would begin in the same way, and this prompted a discussion of other familiar text types, including traditional tales, recounts and procedural texts.

To help the children test their predictions, Jemima read the first few sentences from several familiar Dreaming stories. As she did so, one of the children recorded the opening line on a large piece of paper displayed at the front of the group. With this list in front of them, the children discussed the similarities and differences in story beginnings, deciding that while the beginnings were often similar, their structure might vary.

After working together as a whole class, the children were given a variety of small group tasks which were to be completed over several sessions. These tasks (described below) were all related in some way to the children's developing understanding of Dreaming stories, and focused on the one they had shared most recently — 'How the Birds Got Their Colours', as told by Mary Albert of the Bardi people in Western Australia.

SMALL GROUP TASKS

1. Reconstruct a passage of text at the computer.
Jemima had prepared different versions of the text to match the needs of each of the small groups. Each day, when small group work began, she would open the file prepared for the group using the computer that day.

2. Plan a film strip.
A film strip stencilled on a sheet of A3 paper provided children with a means of recording the key events from the text in the correct sequence.

3. Make a board game.
Once again a stencilled A3 sheet provided children with a framework. Their game had to relate to the story and they were required to use their knowledge of procedural texts to write instructions and rules.

4. Create a story map.
Children were provided with large sheets of blank paper and encouraged to work with a partner. They had already had lots of experience in creating story maps.

L _ _ _, l _ _ _ a _ _ i _ t _ _
D _ _ _ _ _ _ _ _, w _ _ _ t _ _
l _ _ _ a _ _ a _ _ _ _ _ _
w _ _ _ b _ _ _ _ m _ _ _, a _ _
t _ _ b _ _ _ _ w _ _ _ b _ _ _ _,
a _ _ o _ _ c _ _ _ _ _.

Long, long ago in _ _ _
Dreamtime, when _ _ _
land _ _ _ animals
w _ _ _ being made, all
_ _ _ birds were b _ _ ck,
_ _ _ one colour.

Two of the passages that Jemima prepared for the text reconstruction task. The number and type of clues she provided depended on the needs of the group.

The language session ended with a whole class sharing time. This gave the children an opportunity to talk about strategies used at the computer, as well as sharing completed work from other activities.

Using the text completion software

Groups at the computer engaged in much discussion about possible solutions. The software they were using worked in such a way that if an incorrect letter was typed in, it would not remain on the screen; that is, only letters that made up the missing words would be accepted by the program.

The following discussion took place between a group of three boys, for whom Jemima had prepared a passage showing only the initial letter of each word. (This text is given in boxes at appropriate points below.) From observation she knew that these boys were all confident readers who enjoyed a challenge. Their efforts would also be supported by the environmental print that had been generated from class discussions about Dreaming stories and displayed around the room.

> L _ _ _ , l _ _ _ a _ _ i _ t _ _ D _ _ _ _ _ _ _ _ , w _ _ _
>
> *Long, long ago in the Dreamtime, when*

Chris is operating the keyboard while David and Mark look on . . .

DAVID: Look — 'Long long ago in the Dreamtime when . . .'
(He correctly predicts the first seven words; then there is a silence while Chris slowly types in all the letters, with Mark helping him to locate some of the keys)

> t _ _ l _ _ _ a _ _ a _ _ _ _ _ _ w _ _ _ b _ _ _ _ m _ _ _ ,
>
> *the land and animals were being made,*

DAVID: *(pointing to the first word in the next sequence)* 'the'.
MARK: That's 'are'. *(He points to the third word)*
(Chris types in 'r' but it doesn't work)
DAVID: Try 'and'.
(Chris types in 'and')
What's the word before 'and'? *(He points to the second word in this sequence)*
CHRIS: I'm going to try all the vowels to see which one works. *(He types in 'a' after 'l', which proves to be correct)*
DAVID: 'land'.
(Chris types in 'nd' to finish 'land')
MARK: 'land and . . .'? *(He leans across Chris and types in 'n', which is correct)*
DAVID: 'animals' . . .
(Chris finishes typing in 'animals')
'were being made'.
MARK: It's easy when all the first letters are there. You can work out the words.

> a _ _ t _ _ b _ _ _ _ w _ _ _ b _ _ _ _ , a _ _ o _ _ c _ _ _ _ _ .
>
> *all the birds were black, all one colour.*

	(Chris moves the cursor to the beginning of the next group of words)
DAVID:	'and the birds'.
	(Chris types in 'n' but it doesn't work)
MARK:	Try 'are'.
	(Chris types in 'r' but that doesn't work either)
DAVID:	'the birds'.
	(Chris skips over 'a _ _' and types in 'the birds were')
DAVID:	Bright?
CHRIS:	No! 'black', 'cos in the beginning they had to be. *(He types in 'black')*

Jemima had been listening to the boys working. She noticed that David was providing most of the ideas and that all his suggestions were whole words; he was combining the first letter clues with his own sense of the meaning of the text. She was surprised by the level of his contribution as she considered both Mark and Chris to be more confident readers.

By recording the conversations that went on during this type of activity, Jemima could analyse the range of reading strategies the children were able to use. For example, David was able to draw on his familiarity with the structure of Dreaming stories to correctly predict the words in the opening line. He continued to predict whole words rather than morphemes throughout the session (as Jemima had heard at the time), and he was continually making meaning. Even when his suggestions were incorrect, he managed to identify a syntactically appropriate substitution: for example, towards the end he suggested 'bright' rather than 'black'. Chris provided the correct word here by referring back to his contextual knowledge of the story: 'No! "black", 'cos in the beginning they had to be.'

Chris also demonstrated effective strategies, such as reading on (forward referencing) when he did not know a word. Thus when the group could not predict 'all', he took up a suggestion from David and moved on to type in the next phrase, 'the birds were'. However, Mark was guessing words based on their initial sound and length. He was not relating individual words to the meaning of the whole text. For example, he twice guessed 'are' when he saw a three-letter word beginning with 'a', but in neither case was it a syntactically appropriate choice. So while he gave the impression of being a good reader when given a complete text, he demonstrated here that he had a good deal of difficulty in reconstructing text.

Jemima was able to use the information she gained from observing this interaction to plan learning experiences to cater for each child's needs and strengths.

Trying it out

- Modify the starting screen to suit users' needs. Always supply beginners with plenty of significant clues to the meaning of the text; ensuring a degree of success is essential to avoid frustration.

- Model appropriate strategies by 'thinking out loud' when introducing children to the software.
- Encourage children to use the software in pairs or small groups rather than individually. Working together to reconstruct a text prompts them to share their knowledge of language with each other as they make and discuss suggestions. Varying the composition of groups allows them to see a variety of readers at work.
- Provide text completion activities to motivate reluctant readers. Children of all ages are attracted to the game environment created by this type of software. Even those who are usually unable or unwilling to respond to printed text may be drawn into the reconstruction process. A further incentive for reluctant readers is that, unlike pencil and paper cloze, the process leaves no lasting evidence of their mistakes. Incorrect predictions disappear from the screen, giving users immediate feedback about their responses but leaving no record of errors.
- Listen to group discussions to assess children's learning. When children are making suggestions and describing their ideas, it's an ideal opportunity to find out what is going on inside their heads.
- Plan a sharing time after all children have used the software. Help them to make the strategies they used explicit. Perhaps a chart could be created listing possible strategies, such as leaving words out and reading on, re-reading, and predicting words on the basis of contextual, structural and letter/sound clues.
- Link the strategies discussed to other aspects of the class reading program: e.g. *How could these strategies help when you are reading and come to a word that you don't know?*
- Encourage children to speculate on possible alternative versions of the text. This will usually stimulate a discussion on why the author chose specific words or phrases.

Designing concept keyboard overlays

Reading as problem solving

A concept keyboard is an alternative input device which may be used instead of, or as well as, the standard computer keyboard. It is an A3-size touch-sensitive board divided into 128 cells, each of which sends a signal to the computer when pressed. Cells can be programmed separately or linked to adjacent cells, allowing the size and shape of response areas to be varied. The concept keyboard was originally designed to provide easier access to the computer for children with special learning needs who could not use the standard keyboard. Now it is often used to provide support for developing readers and writers.

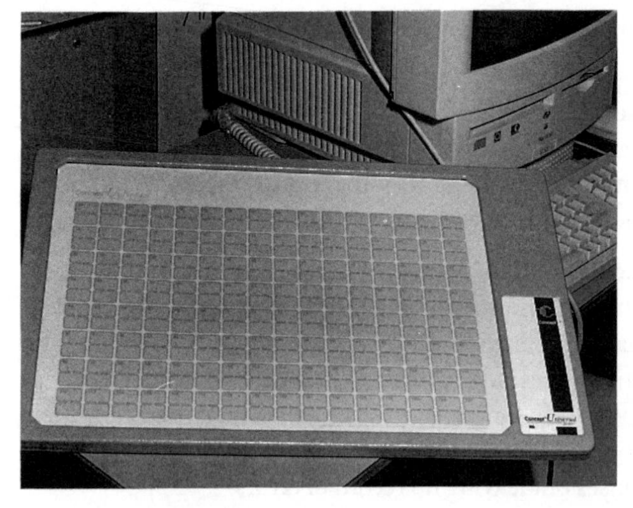

A concept keyboard divided into 128 cells. In programming adjacent cells can be linked together in any pattern.

Using a concept keyboard requires an overlay. This is simply a sheet of paper placed on top of the keyboard to show what letter, word or phrase each response area represents. Appropriate graphics can be added too. By selecting words and phrases in the desired order, developing readers and writers can create their own text, even though they may not be able to write or type the text independently. The words and phrases selected will appear on the computer screen and may then be printed. In this way the use of a concept keyboard can help to scaffold the writing process.

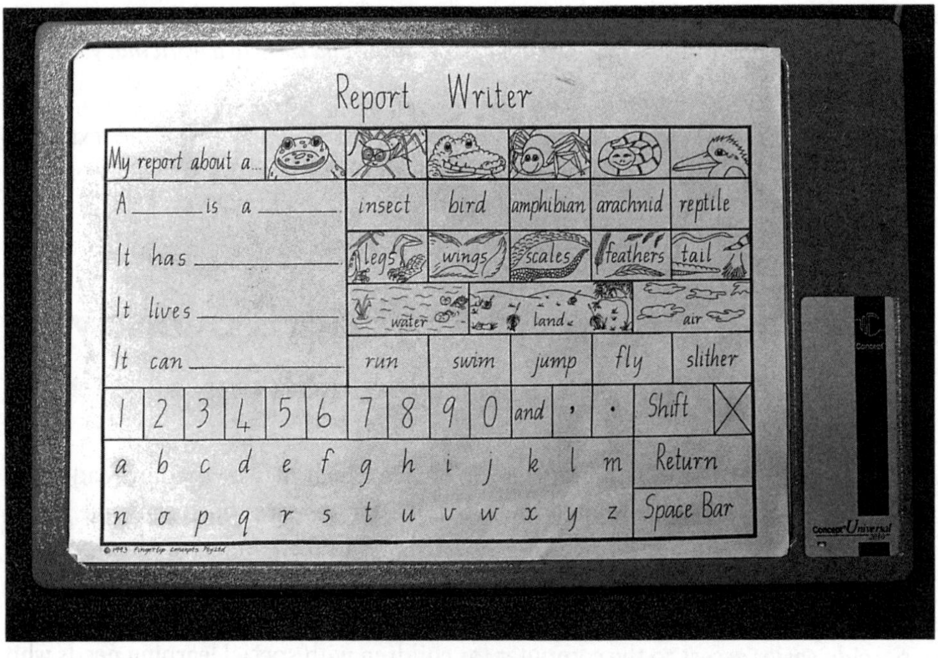

An overlay placed over a concept keyboard to show what letter, word or phrase each area of the keyboard represents.

The concept keyboard can only be used with compatible software. Some software packages include ready-made overlays and offer the option of using either the standard keyboard or the concept keyboard. Alternatively, overlays can be designed by the teacher or by groups of children. Then the response areas can be made as large or small as needed to suit the children who will be using it. Pictures may be added to support developing readers, and it's also possible to have the text in a language other than English.

Once an overlay has been designed on paper, the response areas must be programmed into a computer equipped with the appropriate software. The programming is an easy job and can be done simply by following the on-screen instructions. The information is then saved as a file, which must be opened in order to use that particular overlay.

Response areas can easily be programmed by the teacher or groups of children using the appropriate software.

The design of concept keyboard overlays can provide older children with a stimulating context for problem solving. If the user is to be able to produce a meaningful piece of text without frequent recourse to the alphabet keys, an overlay must include appropriate words and phrases. Often in early drafts children tend to include only nouns and verbs, and it is not until they try to use the overlay to create a piece of text that they become aware of the need to include other parts of speech.

Classroom story

The eleven- and twelve-year-old children in Cheryl's class had spent the final school term engaged in a personal development unit — 'What is it like to be twelve?' — which stimulated much discussion and provided many opportunities for reading and writing. Some of the most stimulating activities grew out of the shared reading of Katherine Paterson's novel *Bridge to Terabithia*.

Cheryl had selected this text as it raised a variety of social issues relevant to the class focus on relationships and human sexuality. The children were so inspired by the book that they wanted to explore the ideas it suggested in much greater depth. So Cheryl planned a range of cross-curriculum activities based on issues identified by the children. As the class had regular access to three computers and a printer, a range of computer-based activities was included.

Several of the activities were done in small groups of three or four, and group members stayed together even when working on individual tasks. These groups were social and, by the children's choice, nearly all of mixed gender. A strong focus on cooperative group work throughout the year had enabled the children to identify peers with whom they could work productively, and by the final term all groups were well-balanced and harmonious. However, Cheryl still gave regular reminders about the importance of equal contribution and collaboration towards a shared goal, and these were usually sufficient to prompt the children to negotiate appropriate roles within their own groups. When programming the concept keyboard, for example, a group of three would divide tasks equally among themselves, with one reading from their draft keyboard overlay, another keying in the text and the third using the mouse to position the cursor.

The activities Cheryl had planned involved problem solving, with many possible responses to each task. Each activity was also designed to send the children back to the ideas or language of the book. For instance, in order to construct a keyboard overlay for writing a synopsis, children needed to identify the main characters and key events in the story to ensure they were provided for on the overlay. Further examples of the planned activities are given in the table opposite.

Using concept keyboards

When Cheryl had first introduced the concept keyboard to her class, she had selected an overlay from a commercial set called *The Australiana Pack* (see photo on p. 48). The children had used it to create reports about specific animals. The design was flexible enough to provide support for several children with learning difficulties, allowing them to create a factual report independently, as well as offering scope for a group of gifted and talented children, who used the alphabet keys to add their own words and phrases.

Concept keyboard activities offered the children many opportunities for problem solving as they explored issues related to sentence structure (e.g. what content words, parts of speech and punctuation were needed) and decided what other functions were necessary (e.g. delete, space). Once they had gained some experience, Cheryl

FIRST SET OF ACTIVITIES	FOLLOW-UP ACTIVITIES
Design a concept keyboard overlay The goal of this small group activity was to design an overlay that would allow users to construct a synopsis of the book.	*Program the design into the computer* Groups had to program their overlay designs into the computer and then test them by attempting to create a synopsis of the story.
Edit and refine the overlay Overlays had to be edited and refined in the light of trials (including a trial by the teacher).	*Write a synopsis* After a group had finalised their design, they gave the overlay to another group to try out.
Write a set of 'thinking' questions The task was to devise questions that would ask the reader to give an opinion rather than reproduce information.	*Responding and evaluating* Each child was given another child's set of questions to respond to and then evaluate.
Draw Terabithia Children were given a passage of text to read and then had to draw their own interpretation of Terabithia.	*Colour the drawing* The task was to colour the drawing from the previous session using a range of crayons.
Design a bridge to Terabithia Another small group task was to design and construct a 'Lego' bridge that would be safer than the rope used by the characters in the story.	*Bridge-building — a new challenge* The design brief for this session was to construct from limited materials a longer bridge that would safely span the creek in times of flood. Once groups were happy with their design, they had to write a procedural text explaining how it was made.
Construct a sociogram Children were given the names of the main characters on a worksheet and had to arrange them to illustrate the relationships between the characters.	*Ode to Leslie* The task here was to write a poem from the main character's point of view, describing how he felt about the loss of his best friend, Leslie. The writing was done in small groups at the computer, using the text facility on *Kid Pix 2*.
Write a book report to share with other readers Children were guided by a prepared worksheet asking for details about the setting, characters, plot, ending, etc.	*Complete a character study* A prompted writing program at the computer (which allows the teacher to enter a series of questions) helped groups to structure their writing about the character of Leslie.

Small group and individual tasks related to Bridge to Terabithia.

set them the task of assisting their Kindergarten buddies to use concept keyboards for writing, using commercial overlays. This gave the Year Six children an opportunity to consolidate their own understandings.

When the children first began designing their own overlays, there was no pressure to program them into the computer. At this stage the emphasis was on the design process. However, when the children started to use the computer, they also needed time to try out their designs and edit them.

Joyce Ann	Miss Edmonds	Leslie	May Belle	Jess	Janice	P.T.	Bill
Katherine Paterson				found	forest	to	Bridge to Terabithia
friend	sister	creek	swing	discovered	in rain	from	
imagine	queen	kingdom	rope	Terabithia	king	secret	loves
bridge	Brenda	Ellie	Miss Bessy	Burke	Aarons	dry	wet
a b	c d	e f	g h	i j	k l	m n	o p
q r	s t	u v	w x	y z	space	. shift	delete

First draft of the overlay design.

The first step in designing the *Bridge to Terabithia* overlays was to work with pencil and paper, each group deciding what text and what graphics were needed. Once their design had been drafted onto an A3 sheet, the group would move to the computer. There, using a software program called *Intercept*, they programmed the design into the computer and saved it as a file. The next step was to try using the overlay to construct a synopsis of the book and make any alterations they found necessary.

When the children in a group were happy with their design, they asked Cheryl to test it out. This is the synopsis she created from the design shown above:

> *Jess Aarons loved Leslie Burke. Jess and Leslie found a secret forest. They called it Terabithia. Leslie was the queen and Jess was the king of Terabithia. Leslie went to Terabithia on her own. She used the rope to swing across the creek. She fell into the creek and drowned.*

However, as Cheryl put the synopsis together, she found that she often needed to use the alphabet keys to type in words that had not been included on the overlay. She drew the children's attention to this and they noted which words were missing, as well as some which had not been used. In particular, they identified a need for prepositions, pronouns and conjunctions (previously they had concentrated mainly on content words). So they deleted some words like 'wet' and 'dry' from their draft and added others like 'they', 'on' and 'and'.

Joyce Ann | Miss Edmonds | Leslie | May Belle | Jess | Janice | P.T. | Bill
Katherine Paterson | found | forest | went | called | Bridge to Terabithia
friend | sister | creek | swing | discovered | in | rain | from
imagine | queen | drown | fell | rope | Terabithia | king | secret | loves
bridge | Brenda | Ellie | Miss Bessy | they | he | she | to | the | and | is | on
a | b | c | d | e | f | g | h | i | j | k | l | m | n | o | p
q | r | s | t | u | v | w | x | y | z | space | . | shift | delete

Second draft of the overlay design.

Having adjusted their paper overlay, the group returned to the computer to edit their file. The overlay was then ready for another group to try out.

Trying it out

- Spend time developing cooperative skills. This will help to ensure that children gain maximum benefit from working in small groups at the computer.
- Help children to develop a range of problem-solving strategies. Design activities that allow ideas to be tried out and modified and for which there is a range of possible solutions.
- Give children responsibility for deciding whether or not they have been successful in completing a task. Depending on the software selected, computer-based activities have great potential for promoting independent learning.
- Provide opportunities for children to explore commercial overlays before they attempt designs of their own.
- Emphasise the design process rather than the finished product when children are creating their first overlays. There is no need to program these first designs into the computer.
- Allow time for children to test and edit their designs. Once they are happy with them, overlays should be tried out by other groups.

- Encourage children to compare finished writing created with commercial overlays to finished writing created from their own designs. Ask them to identify any differences between the two and to consider how they might be explained.

USING CONCEPT KEYBOARDS WITH BEGINNING READERS AND WRITERS

As mentioned previously, concept keyboards provide an excellent means of scaffolding the writing process for developing readers and writers. A few guidelines are suggested below:

- When you are using commercial overlays, ensure that children are familiar with the text and that it is relevant to their own experience.
- Involve children in selecting the text when you are preparing your own overlays for scaffolding their writing.
- Use images to help children identify key words and phrases.
- Support the initial use of overlays by involving older buddies who are familiar with concept keyboards.

USING CONCEPT KEYBOARDS WITH CHILDREN WHO HAVE SPECIAL LEARNING NEEDS

- Plan the size of response areas and the size of the text to match the child's individual needs. For example, a child who has problems with fine motor coordination will need larger response areas. Similarly, the size, style and colour of the text may be critical for a child with a visual impairment.
- Contact a computer education consultant or a special needs consultant to find out about appropriate software. There is a range of programs specifically designed for children with special learning needs.

Issues to consider when planning to enhance reading

Many different types of software programs besides the two described in this chapter have a component that may contribute to children's reading development. Some of them are identified in the following discussion of relevant issues.

How can computer-based learning experiences be designed to cater for readers with a range of different needs?

Many software programs allow the teacher to make modifications to suit learners' individual needs. For example, when Jemima was using a text completion program, she was able to prepare different passages of text and also adjust the number of clues available on the opening screen to provide more or less challenge for different groups in her classroom.

Other types of software allow children to determine their own response: for example, the software used to program concept keyboard overlays allows them to be made as simple or as complex as desired. This type of software is available for most major brands of computer.

Word processing software also allows children to work at their own level. When the children in Cheryl's class were writing the 'Ode to Leslie', some groups produced short, simple verse, while others explored the possibilities of haiku and cinquains. Nevertheless all of them were using the text facility on *Kid Pix 2* — the same draw/paint program as Anna used in her classroom (Chapter 3). There too it allowed the children to be successful at any level, with some happily making scribble patterns as they explored the various tools and others producing complex designs, pictures or written text.

In addition, the structure of groups at the computer can be varied to match the needs, strengths and interests of learners. For example, the children in Cheryl's class worked cooperatively in mixed ability friendship groups. This grouping method was particularly successful; children brought along different needs and strengths and happily assisted each other to complete a range of different tasks.

Sometimes, however, interaction between teacher and children at the computer is the most effective way of scaffolding their learning. Once the children in Cheryl's class had had time to draft and edit their concept keyboard overlays, she worked with them, constructing her own synopsis from their designs and guiding them towards appropriate modifications. At this stage groups had gone as far as they could by themselves and needed her help to refine their work. Similarly, Anna worked with small groups at the computer to develop their skills in cooperative problem solving, providing the level of assistance each child needed within a meaningful context.

What is the role of talking software?

Recent developments in the sound capability of computer technology have led to an increasing number of 'talking' programs appearing on the market. Depending on the situation in which they are used, such programs may bring advantages and disadvantages.

'Talking word processors' can alert users to questions of spelling, helping them to make judgements about particular cases and also see where the wrong word may have been typed in. Some word processing programs will respond to voice input; if the user says a word that he or she can't spell, the computer will include the word. At this stage, however, the software can only handle individual words, not passages of text. These word processors will also 'read' back what has been written.

Electronic texts or 'talking books' have become very popular in recent years, with CD ROM technology producing vast improvements in the quality of the speech. Programs include both narrative and factual texts. There are also quite a few bilingual programs available, which have the advantage of allowing some second language learners to hear the text in English or their first language.

Talking books usually offer users the choice of hearing the whole text or of selecting passages or individual words to hear again. Some of the more recent titles also allow innovation on the text. Talking books read the written text, but the 'talking' may include additional dialogue which users can select, as well as directions or prompts which offer support to developing readers and may allow them to work through a text independently.

One of the most frequently cited advantages of talking books is their capacity to motivate reluctant readers through the use of sound, graphics and animation (Shand 1994). In addition, reading along with the computer may help to improve a child's fluency and pronunciation. (See also Chapter 8, where children create their own talking books.)

While talking software can provide support for emergent readers, there may be disadvantages for children from language backgrounds other than English. For example, exposure to a variety of accents or dialects may be a source of confusion for some. Generally, however, the advantages of hearing the text pronounced and seeing illustrations which support meaning far outweigh the disadvantages of variations in accent.

Some draw/paint software allows the user to add his or her own voice and other sound effects via a microphone. This facility also allows the teacher to add instructions, which may be more useful for some children than the standard prompts and directions provided in commercial software.

What criteria should guide the selection and use of talking books in a reading program?

Although talking books are increasingly popular, you should take care in selecting them to support your reading program, for some offer little more than an electronic page-turning facility. Talking books should be used to complement other learning experiences, not because they contain colourful graphics or clever animations. Always apply to them the same stringent standards as you would to any other piece of literature. Dennis Mike (1994) suggests the following set of selection criteria:

interactivity – users should be able to interact with the text to develop further understanding

speed – it should not take long to move from one page to the next

clarity – the screen layout should be clear and allow intuitive use by young children

speech/sound – the sound should be of high quality (some recent programs allow users to input their own voice in certain places)

graphics – these should be clear, colourful and relevant to the text; don't be taken in by clever animations if they add nothing to the reader's understanding

second language support – quite a few programs have a second language option which is easily activated

integration of writing – some recent titles incorporate writing activities, thus allowing talking, listening, reading and writing to be integrated

teacher control – there should be some facility to adapt the program to cater for individuals (e.g. by putting more or less text on each page)

support materials – the program should include a printed version of the text and a teacher's guide.

How can the use of computer-based learning experiences help teachers to assess children's reading development?

Clearly a variety of reading skills can be developed by using different software programs. Listening to children's discussions and interacting directly with them as they use the software provides many opportunities for assessing their reading development. For example, the type of predictions children make while they are using text completion software may reveal a great deal about their understanding of sentence structure and meaning. Some children in Jemima's classroom who were considered to be confident readers of complete texts experienced considerable difficulty when called on to reconstruct a passage of text.

Similarly, Cheryl was able to assess the children's understanding of the book they had shared as they worked on constructing a synopsis with the concept keyboard. The design process also revealed the children's knowledge of sentence construction when they considered what types of words would be needed to write a clear and concise synopsis.

In Tom's classroom, described in the next chapter, where the children had to read on-screen clues in an adventure game, he could assess their ability to interpret the information provided by listening to them discussing their progress through the game.

The last three chapters, which describe children working on the reading-writing connection within electronic texts, suggest further opportunities for assessment. In Chapter 7, for example, the children's computer-based reading and writing about the solar system gave Christine many chances to assess their skills in locating, selecting and interpreting information. And, in Chapter 9, Shirley was able to ask the children to explain their interpretations of character and story implicit in the questions they sent on-line to Rich and Bee (the central figures in Alison Lester's *Imagine*) and assess their ability to justify them.

For further reading, viewing or playing

Books and articles

Fatouros, C., Downes, T. & Blackwell, S. 1994, *In Control: Young Children Learning with Computers*, Social Science Press, Wentworth Falls, NSW.

Hawkridge, D. & Vincent, T. 1992, *Learning Difficulties and Computers: Access to the Curriculum*, Taylor and Francis, Philadelphia.

Pipe, D. 1994, 'Literacy at your fingertips', *On-Line*, vol. 10, no. 3, pp 12-13.

Scrimshaw, P. 1993, 'Text completion programs', in P. Scrimshaw (ed.), *Language, Classrooms and Computers*, Routledge, New York.

Shand, C. 1994, 'The new entertainment medium: books on CD?', in S. Wawrzyniak & L. Samootin (eds.), *Ask Me Why? Proceedings of the 10th Annual New South Wales Computers in Education Conference*, NSW Computer Education Group, Sydney.

Commercially produced overlays

Jarred, A. & Roelofs, N. 1994, *Designer Overlays: A Whole Language Approach for Computer Touch Boards*. Titles in this series include *Kindy Pack*, *Junior Pack*, *The Australiana Pack* and *The Dragon Pack*. For further information, contact Fingertip Concepts on (09) 227 5942, KTM Consultant on (02) 552 4413, or Alto Computers on (07) 852 2480.

Software

TEXT COMPLETION SOFTWARE

Text Detective (Macintosh).

CONCEPT KEYBOARD SOFTWARE

Intellikeys (Macintosh, Windows, DOS).

TALKING BOOKS (descriptions adapted from Shand 1994)

Discis Series (Macintosh/MPC CD ROM). Programs in this series present a screen image resembling an open book. Illustrations are mostly taken from the printed text; there is no animation but frequent background music. Teachers can customize the software in a variety of ways. Titles include *Aesop's Fables*, *The Paper Bag Princess*, *The Tale of Peter Rabbit*, *Moving Gives Me a Stomach Ache* and *Scary Poems for Rotten Kids*.

Living Book Series (Macintosh/MPC CD ROM). This series makes much more use of images, sound and animation than the Discis series. There is great potential for interaction with the images but possibilities for customising the software are limited. Titles include *Arthur's Teacher Trouble*, *Just Grandma and Me*, *The Tortoise and the Hare*, *Ruff's Bone* and *The New Kid on the Block* (a collection of poetry).

The Ugly Duckling (Macintosh/MPC CD ROM, Windows). Some songs and chants are included.

WiggleWorks (Macintosh CD ROM). This program incorporates writing activities.

Writing

Word processing programs enable writers to input, edit, save, format and print text. Research has shown that their use has an impact on both the quality and quantity of the texts produced, which tend to be longer, neater and more 'error-free' than handwritten texts (Cochran-Smith 1991). However, word processing programs by themselves can effect little improvement in the fundamental quality of children's writing. For example, children who have problems sequencing events in a recount or identifying the steps in a procedure may be able produce a longer piece of text with less spelling errors on a word processor, but the experience won't challenge them to reconsider the structure of their writing. What they need is to spend time conferencing what they have written with adults or more capable peers — the sort of people who can help them to see writing as a process of making meaning and communicating this meaning to others. In the same way, of course, children need experienced support to help them make effective use of the extensive editing features offered by word processing software.

Word processing programs usually provide for input via a standard computer keyboard, but there are other options that are particularly suitable for younger children or those with special learning needs. For example, the concept keyboard (Chapter 4) can be used to assist developing writers in a number of ways: keyboard overlays can display letters in alphabetical order, or specific words or phrases (perhaps accompanied by a picture), or words in a language other than English. Some current word processors also have a limited capacity for speech input, whereby the user says a word and the computer inserts that word into the text.

The editing capacity of word processing programs is perhaps their most powerful feature, for it allows all kinds of revisions without any need to laboriously rewrite (or retype) the whole text. Users can try out different words or sentence constructions, or even play around with the organisation of ideas within the text.

Words, phrases, sentences or whole blocks of text can be easily copied, moved or deleted. Thus the task of editing and refining a piece of writing becomes much less onerous, and children are likely to edit their text more thoroughly and take more risks than when writing by hand. In addition, text can be saved at any point, either to be worked on later or to preserve different versions. Indeed, several versions of a piece of writing can be printed and conferenced, allowing the writer to see the effect of various changes. More sophisticated editing features include spelling and grammar checkers and thesauruses.

Formatting includes the modification of such features as text alignment (justified on the left or right margin, on both margins, or centred), the style and size of the font (or typeface) and the page layout (paragraphs of text, columns or tables). A text can be printed at any stage from first to final draft. A printed version of the first draft can be used to conference and edit the writing before on-screen editing (some people find it easier to edit a printed version than to edit directly on screen). Once editing is completed, a final copy can be printed with appropriate font sizes, styles and formatting.

Depending on the software used, borders and graphics may also be added before printing, or children may add their own hand-drawn illustrations at a later stage. Alternatively, if drawing is the most important part of the text (as it may be for young writers), a paint/draw program may be the most appropriate choice. Most paint/draw programs include a limited word processing facility, allowing the user to move easily between drawing and writing. This is often crucial for developing writers, whose written text tends to emerge from their drawings and may lead back to extensions of them (Blackstock & Miller 1992).

Word processing with young children

Classroom story

Nada decided that by introducing her six- and seven-year-old students to word processing she could further promote their developing writing skills. Her school had a computer room with nine computers and several printers, to which she had access. There were also a few stand-alone computers available, which were shared amongst the teachers who wanted to use them in their classrooms.

Nada had a range of goals in mind, based on her observation of the children's needs, strengths and interests. Most importantly, she wanted the children to maintain their positive attitudes towards writing while being receptive to suggestions for improvements and extensions in their work. She was concerned that many of the children could orally relate their ideas for a narrative or a recount but were often unable or unwilling to translate these thoughts into written text. She believed that in some cases this was due to limited handwriting skills, whilst other children seemed to be put off by the prospect of rewriting at the editing and publishing stages. The use of a word processor would help by eliminating the need for rewriting, as well as allowing children with poor handwriting to produce a neat final copy.

Nada also believed that small group work around the computer would encourage children to engage in more shared composition as they talked about what they wanted to say and shared the keying in. Moreover, having the text displayed clearly on the computer monitor would make the writing process more public, encouraging an instant response from the group (and passers-by) as the text progressed.

Introducing the software

The first session in the computer room began with a whole class demonstration. Using the word processing component of a program called *ClarisWorks*, Nada helped the children to identify the letter keys, the space bar, the arrow keys and the delete key, though she didn't discuss use of the shift and return keys at this stage. She showed how just a light pressure was enough to operate any of the keys. The font size and style were pre-selected; Nada had chosen the Foundation font (installed on the computers using a program called *Aussie School Fonts*) as it would help to reinforce correct letter shapes.

Initially the children worked at the computers in friendship groups of three, as Nada believed that this would provide the most supportive context for them to become familiar with the hardware and software. Each computer group was asked to work together to create a written text. There was no pressure to complete it, but Nada did insist that each member of the group had a turn at using the keyboard.

All the children were delighted with their results, regardless of whether they finished or not. Nada noted that some of them who normally wrote without leaving spaces between words seemed to have overcome that problem at the computer, where the act of pressing a key to create a space appeared to make the convention more concrete for them. Using computers also reinforced the children's ideas of the directionality of print, since the movement from left to right occurred automatically as they typed in their texts.

Some children expressed a need for capital letters and full stops during the session, and so Nada introduced these keyboard features to individuals and groups as the need arose. When the issue of punctuation came up for discussion in a whole class sharing time afterwards, she decided to cover these features with all the children next time.

last nit my aunty
has sum kittns but i
hasnt sin it. by
ryan mele madeline.

A first draft: this group quickly realised the need for capital letters.

The second session in the computer room gave the children another opportunity to finish a piece of writing and to print their work. Some groups printed several pieces of writing (seeming to delight in the novelty of using the printer), while others spent the whole session still exploring the keyboard.

Nada asked the children who had learnt to use full stops and capital letters during the first session to share their knowledge with the others. In fact the children soon learnt that if they were having any sort of problem they should ask the groups on either side of them before calling the teacher. This strategy helped them to consolidate their developing skills and understandings — to say nothing of the positive effect on their self-esteem!

By the third session all children were encouraged to use full stops and capital letters appropriately. Working collaboratively in friendship groups, the children with poor writing skills or those who lacked confidence in their writing ability were clearly benefiting from the group interaction. One child, six-year-old Jason, whose poor fine-motor coordination meant that he had great difficulty in producing legible handwriting, was particularly excited by the use of the word processing program.

One of Jason's handwritten texts.

Indeed he was so proud of his first word-processed text that he carried it with him wherever he went, showing it to every teacher, helper or child he met. He even had it for 'news' (in a somewhat tattered state) a week after it had been written.

my anti has a babi
bat my litow sitsa lix
it

Using a word processor helped Jason to communicate more effectively with written text.

Nevertheless Nada was concerned that the more talented writers were still producing texts only one or two sentences long. She wondered if they were spending too much time helping others, or if they were so keen to have a printed copy of their work that they were sacrificing extended writing to produce a number of print-outs quickly. So, in the fourth session, she grouped several of them together and set all the children a more specific task, asking them to write a letter to a previous class member who had moved to a new school. While all groups managed to complete this task successfully, the talented writers still needed more encouragement to work to their full potential. Nada planned to continue grouping them together for particular tasks and also to negotiate some more challenging projects with them.

Now that all the children had gained some experience in using the software, Nada planned to shift the emphasis towards developing writing skills. In the immediate future, as the children were learning to write recounts, the sessions at the computer would focus on the structure of this genre. Nada wanted the children to view the computer and word processing software as a means of developing their writing rather than as an end in itself.

To gain the most benefit from using word processing software, Nada believed that it was essential for the children to use the computer at the composing stage, rather than merely 'typing up' their handwritten drafts. She also believed that reluctant writers like Jason needed more opportunities to use the word processor. Accordingly she decided to negotiate with other staff to have one of the school's stand-alone computers in her classroom to supplement the rostered computer room time.

Trying it out

➤ Select software to match the needs of the children. For young children, a draw/paint program with a word processing facility may be most suitable, as it allows them to move back and forth between drawing and written text.

  For developing writers, a simple program that allows large type and has few menu options (or allows some to be hidden) would be most appropriate. Beware, however, of software that places limits on the length of the text.

  Older children or more experienced writers may benefit from features such as spell checkers, thesauruses and more sophisticated formatting options. If you want children to be able to write in their first language, there are also word processing programs available that allow for the use of non-English characters.

  For some children, a game-type program which helps them find their way around the keyboard may also be useful.

➤ Consider the level of resources available. For example, if you only have access to one computer in your classroom, it's impractical for each child to work on a piece of individual writing. Other options include cooperative composing, chain stories (where small groups add a sentence or paragraph to a piece of writing that then becomes a whole class effort), or planned access for specific groups of children. It may also be possible to negotiate with other staff to have access to several computers for a specified length of time.

➤ Make use of appropriate grouping strategies. Friendship grouping, peer tutoring and buddy systems are all useful strategies, allowing children to share the construction of a piece of text in a supportive environment. Remember, however, that grouping strategies may need to be changed as children's needs change and different writing purposes arise. Consider too the needs of individuals: some children work well in groups; others feel the need to have total control of the text being written.

- Provide opportunities initially for children to explore features of the word processing software. It's essential to give them time to familiarise themselves with these features before they undertake a specific writing task. Although an open-ended task may provide a meaningful context for exploration, the final product should not be emphasised in the early stages.
- Arrange for whole group sharing times after children have spent a while writing at the computer. They can be very valuable, allowing children to learn from each other's discoveries and promoting their self-esteem. They also provide an opportunity to identify individual and whole class needs, strengths and interests for the next session.
- Encourage children to seek help from each other in the first instance. Besides relieving the pressure on you, this will promote their learning and self-esteem.
- Introduce new features of the software as need arises. The need may be confined to one or two individuals or small groups, or may extend to the whole class.
- Encourage risk-taking — mistakes are easily removed. Children can experiment with the effect of different words, different sentence structures, or even a different sequence of ideas. Make sure they understand that they can explore different choices and refine their text without the need for lengthy rewriting.
- Make plans to store writing on disk as well as, or instead of, printing it out. Disks should be labelled and kept in the reading area with other reading materials, and children should be encouraged to read each other's electronic texts as well as their printed ones. Old computers that have become obsolete for most purposes are ideal here; they can be permanently set up in the reading area.

Cooperative composing of factual texts

Using word processing software for teacher demonstrations and small group joint constructions offers many advantages over more traditional methods:

- the public nature of the screen display means that everyone in the group can see the text (provided the size and position of the monitor are appropriate)
- the regularity of the typed text means that it is easy to read
- if the computer has a detachable keyboard which can be passed around, all members of the group can actively contribute to the joint construction

- the facility to cut or copy and paste means that ideas can easily be reorganised without decreasing readability
- access to a printer allows copies of the text to be quickly printed for all members of the group, or for several copies to be displayed around the room.

In the following classroom story, the classroom computer is used for a teacher-led joint construction to revise the key features of the explanation genre. The teacher then provides opportunities for small groups of children to jointly construct their own explanations on laptop computers.

Classroom story

Roslyn was teaching a class of nine- and ten-year-olds. She had one computer and a printer permanently set up in the classroom, and she was also able to book up to three of the school's laptop computers for various sessions during the week. She often borrowed them twice a week during language sessions when the children were doing lots of writing. The children were familiar with the process of collecting the laptops, connecting them to power, saving their stories to disk and printing them out on the classroom printer.

In Term 2 the class was investigating weather patterns and their impact on living things. The children had already studied seasons several years previously. This time around, Roslyn hoped to further develop their understandings of the concepts of climate, change and cycles, and to further demonstrate the dependence of living things on their natural environment.

As part of her English curriculum, Roslyn wanted the children to revisit the genre of explanations. She identified components of the Science unit where it would be appropriate for her to model and jointly construct explanations and for the children to write their own in small groups. She planned to use the classroom computer and word processing software for the demonstrations.

The joint construction sessions came at the end of a module on 'Why do we have different seasons?' During this module children had read factual texts, viewed videos, built models of a tilting earth rotating around the sun, and had many discussions about how the earth rotates on its axis at the same time as rotating around the sun. For the joint construction sessions Roslyn divided the children into three groups. Two groups worked on a wall frieze displaying the key characteristics of each season in various climatic zones, while the third group worked with her constructing the text for an explanation. The group was small enough to allow all the children to see the computer screen and contribute to the joint construction.

With the group gathered around the computer screen, Roslyn asked questions to help the children develop the explanation. She took the opportunity to model ways of cutting and pasting the text as various children argued for the rearrangement of ideas. She reminded the group of the IOU method of editing (work on Information first, Organisation second and Usage last) and used it to edit their text.

Jointly constructing a text using the computer.

As each of the three groups had a turn, print-outs of the jointly constructed texts were made for group members and enlarged versions were hung on the wall. The children annotated their own print-outs to remind them of the structure of the text and the common language features and stored them in their writing folders for future reference.

Over the next few weeks the class worked on such questions as:

How do humans in temperate and arctic zones adapt their agriculture to the seasons?

How do animals, such as penguins and seals, adapt to the arctic seasons?

How do different species of plants adapt to the various seasons in colder climates?

How do reptiles survive winters in colder climates?

During their research the children came across a range of phenomena such as hibernation and bird migration. In class discussions they began to compile a list of questions such as:

Why do snakes hibernate?

Why do some trees loose their leaves in autumn?

Why do birds migrate?

Why do penguins always return to the same island year after year to breed?

As the unit progressed, smaller groups of three students chose one of these questions to research cooperatively. They used a variety of texts in the school library, consulted knowledgeable adults in the community and viewed a number of videos

Small groups cooperatively composing their explanations.

borrowed from the local library. They presented their findings in the form of written explanations, which they composed together around the computer. Again Roslyn organised this stage so that three groups of children worked on their texts on the three laptops, while other groups worked independently on collages displaying images of adaptation.

Each group of three brought all their notes with them to the computer. Their first task was to assign the role of typist and organise themselves so that they could all see the screen clearly. That done, their main task during this first session (as they had been reminded) was to work on the content of their explanation. Roslyn rostered the groups through a four-day cycle, allowing each one about forty minutes at the computer. At the end of the week, when each group had a reasonable draft of their work, she held a whole class session where she revised the structure and common language conventions of explanations. During the following week each group had another turn at the computer to revise their explanation and print out copies of their completed text, ready for publication in a class booklet entitled 'Adapting to the Seasons'.

Trying it out

- Plan regular demonstrations and joint constructions using word processing software. These sessions allow you to demonstrate the editing features of the software within a meaningful context (i.e. as you introduce or revisit particular genres or model general conventions of written text).

- Lead additional small group sessions for children who need more scaffolding. When all eyes are focused on the computer screen rather than on an individual, children can participate in a joint construction without feeling threatened.
- Get older buddies to act as 'typists' for young writers whose keyboard skills are not yet well developed. This will allow the writers to focus on composing their text rather than hunting for keys.
- Use the school's old computers for word processing activities. Many schools have some outmoded computers which are rarely used because they don't have enough memory to run the most recent software or because they don't have colour monitors. These machines are still suitable for word processing and will give you more options for writing tasks. You could also negotiate loans or donations of similar machines from parents or local businesses.
- Prepare a word processing file with appropriate prompts, or select a commercial program designed for this purpose. The prompts should assist children with the overall organisation of text in a specified genre. For example, here are some possible prompts for an explanation:
  - What is the phenomenon you are going to explain? Write this as a question.
  - Write one or two sentences describing this phenomenon.
  - Write your explanation of this phenomenon. Remember to use the present tense.

  The use of this file or an appropriate software program (e.g. *Writer's Toolkit*) could be demonstrated as part of the teacher-led joint construction.

Issues to consider when planning to enhance writing

There is a range of issues to consider when using word processing software with children, some of which arose in the previous classroom stories.

Do children need touch typing skills before using word processing software?

The short answer is no. While children need to develop keyboard awareness in order to use word processing software successfully, they do not need to be able to touch type. Touch typing (a method originally developed for copy typists) is especially useful when large amounts of text need to be entered quickly, but it is not a high priority that children should learn this skill.

The most important features of word processing software for children relate to the composing and editing of text. Nevertheless they will still become frustrated if they have to search for every key, and it's essential to introduce the keyboard and its features systematically. Anticipate what features they will need at any particular stage and give them as much practice time as possible. Practice alone will bring the familiarity that makes the mechanics of keyboard use more or less automatic, allowing them to concentrate on the real tasks of composing and revising. Remember to show them that a light touch will operate each key; 'thumping' isn't necessary!

Group work can help to eliminate some of the frustrations of inexperience; working in pairs or groups of three, children can assist one another to locate the required keys as they compose their text together. There are also a number of other ways of helping children to develop their keyboard awareness.

- ➤ Use whole class sessions to introduce or revise needed features (shift keys, arrow keys, return keys, etc.) and visit small groups to provide reinforcement as necessary.
- ➤ Provide lots of opportunities for children to explore the software for their own or teacher-directed purposes.
- ➤ Make typewriters and obsolete computers or keyboards available in the classroom for exploration or practice.
- ➤ Display keyboard strips on children's desks or elsewhere in the room.
- ➤ Draw or paint a large keyboard somewhere in the playground. Children can use this for hopscotch or spelling games and at the same time become familiar with key locations.
- ➤ Use a word processor sometimes when scribing for young children (e.g. to label pictures or scribe stories that they dictate to you about their drawings). This helps to model the keying in of text, and they can participate by identifying and locating some of the letters needed.
- ➤ Add typing tutor software to the classroom's recreational collection.

Children who have mastered the art of handwriting but have little or no keyboard experience may find hunting for keys during the composing stage very frustrating, especially if they tend to write extended texts. Some basic strategies may assist here:

- left hand on left side of keyboard, right hand on right side and thumb on the space bar (a strip of card may be slotted in between the keys running down the centre of the keyboard to serve as a reminder)
- identify home keys (as in touch typing)
- become familiar with the most commonly used keys — vowels, common consonants, special keys.

If lack of familiarity with the keyboard is causing problems initially, another strategy is to have parent helpers type in children's first drafts, exactly as written, leaving the children free to concentrate on the editing process.

Do you need access to a computer room in order to use word processing software successfully? What other possibilities are there?

In an ideal situation teachers would have access to a computer room or a cluster of computers, as well as having at least one computer permanently set up in the classroom and the option of borrowing several others for specific sessions during the week. Yet though well-equipped schools are now approaching this level of resources, many others are still sharing one computer between several classes.

In most schools extensive individual use of computers is impossible, and in many ways this situation is not educationally desirable. By working cooperatively, children can help each other with planning and drafting their writing, locating required keys, editing and publishing. Cooperative writing also has the advantage of providing a ready-made audience on which to test ideas and second-thoughts.

Computer groups may be structured in various ways, whether the children are in a computer room or using one or more stand-alone computers in the classroom.

Collaborative. When two or three children collaborate to compose a text, the writing process becomes more exciting (and for some less daunting) as they bounce ideas off each other and share the composition and keying-in. This form of grouping can be used in conjunction with a roster system to allow all children to have a turn at the computer. It may also be appropriate when groups are working on a specific project (e.g. the joint construction of explanations in Roslyn's classroom).

Groups may be based on friendship, interest or language background. As mentioned earlier, some word processing programs now provide selection of non-English characters and can be used to allow children from language backgrounds other than English to write in their first language.

Peer tutoring. In this type of grouping a more skilled child acts as a tutor to another child. At the computer it may mean that the tutor is a child who understands the requisite features of the hardware and software and is able to key in the text, while the other child takes the main responsibility for composing. The tutor may also assist with aspects of the writing (e.g. word choice or sentence structure).

Adult-directed. Roslyn used adult-directed groups when she was modelling the process of joint construction to prepare the children for the work they would do in smaller collaborative groups. A computer with a moveable keyboard can be an advantage here, as group members can sit comfortably around the monitor and share the keyboarding.

This kind of grouping may also be appropriate for children who have special learning needs, with the computer providing a context for regular interactions with a support teacher or parent, or perhaps an older buddy.

Regardless of grouping arrangements or location, computer-based writing is essentially a more public form of communication, as the text is displayed on the screen for any passer-by to read. This feature of the computer environment, combined with a cooperative method of grouping, may help to develop children's sense of audience more effectively than an individual pen-and-paper approach.

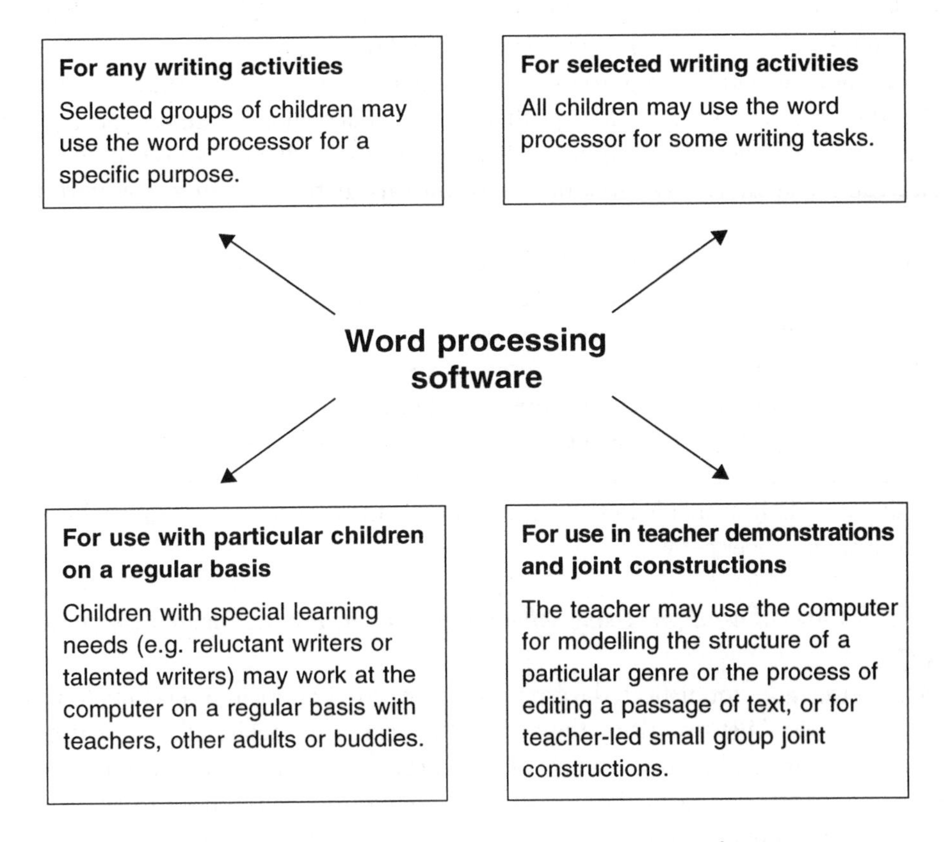

Word processing software may be used in a variety of ways.

How can children be encouraged to focus on the writing process rather than the final print-out? What access to printers is necessary?

When children are first introduced to word processing, the novelty of producing a print-out that looks like 'book writing' may be so great that they opt for a fast result and pay little attention to the quality of their writing. As you'll recall, Nada found this was a problem in the early stages of using word processors with her class, and one way she overcame it was to alter the method of grouping. Once children had spent some time becoming familiar with the hardware and software in their friendship groups, she grouped the talented writers together and set them a specific task. The effect was not immediate (the children were still keen to have their final print-out), but after she had negotiated writing tasks with them and emphasised the goals to be achieved, they gradually spent longer developing and refining their text.

Some children (and adults) find it difficult to edit text on a screen, and so a combination of screen and paper editing may be desirable. Access to a printer is important for this reason, but children don't necessarily need to print their work after each session at the computer. It may be that they only do so when they are ready for final editing or conferencing (which will save paper), though they should back-up their files on another disk to avoid losing work. If access to printers is difficult, then writing can be saved on a disk and printed when one is available.

Children need to have a purpose for refining their text, and it is always important that they can identify an audience (other than members of the composing team) for their writing. When the computer is being used, the audience can respond to the electronic text by typing questions or comments at the end for the writer(s) to consider in later editing.

Over time, with modelling of the editing process and conferencing of draft writing, children will gradually become less obsessed with 'the print-out' and concentrate more on the purpose for their writing. It's vital that they are not misled by the authoritative look of computer-generated print; they must be led to realise that the quality of the content is more important.

A further option is to shift the focus from the printed version of the text to the electronic version, with the printed version as an adjunct. If disk copies of children's writing are made available in the reading corner, the electronic version can be read as well as the paper copy.

What features of word processing software support the pre-writing and composition stages?

Most of the more sophisticated word processing programs include a facility to work in 'outline view' before writing the body of the text. This facility allows the user to create headings for key ideas and move them around to achieve a satisfactory overall structure. It can be particularly useful when children are required to synthesise information from a variety of sources in order to write their own reports.

The first task in using an outliner is to create a list of the major topics to be covered (which may be provided by the teacher). For example, in a report about an animal, the major topics might be:

1. Appearance
2. Habitat
3. Behaviour

The next task is to research information and record details under each of these topic headings. The details should be brief — just a word or a phrase — for then children are more likely to express the information in their own words when they come to writing the report.

The following example, based on one from Anderson-Inman and Zeitz (1994), shows how an outliner can help children to identify areas where they need to find more information. Here more research is needed about the animal's habitat.

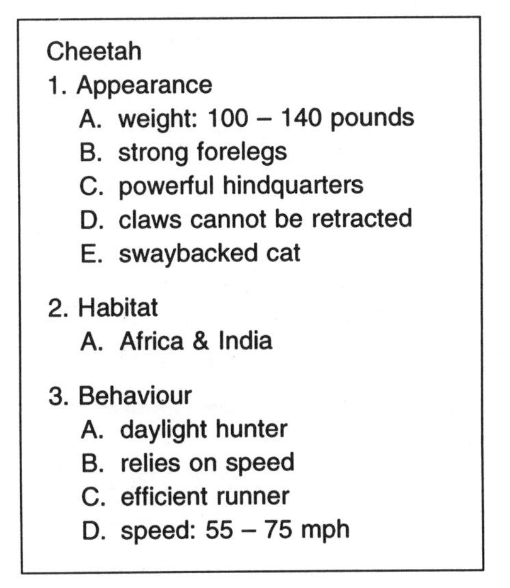

Cheetah
1. Appearance
   A. weight: 100 – 140 pounds
   B. strong forelegs
   C. powerful hindquarters
   D. claws cannot be retracted
   E. swaybacked cat

2. Habitat
   A. Africa & India

3. Behaviour
   A. daylight hunter
   B. relies on speed
   C. efficient runner
   D. speed: 55 – 75 mph

An outliner helps children to organise information before writing.

Once the outline is complete, children expand the information under each of their sub-topics to create the finished report. At this stage of writing, the outliner can help them to reorganise key points in their text via a facility to expand and collapse the headings. Headings can be expanded to see more of the text and collapsed to focus on high-level structure. When a collapsed heading is moved, all associated text moves with it — a feature which makes the reorganisation of ideas considerably easier.

An alternative to using outliners for organising information is software which allows children to create a concept map; *Inspiration* is one such program.

Some software provides support throughout the writing process, from pre-writing stage to final draft, by including a series of steps for the writer to work through. An example is a program called *Writer's Toolkit*, which includes a standard word processor and provides a range of tools to help the writer build a wordbank, take notes, structure ideas, write a draft and proofread the text.

For further reading, viewing or playing

Books and articles

Anderson-Inman, L. & Zeitz, L. 1994, 'Beyond notecards: synthesizing information with electronic study tools', *The Computing Teacher*, vol. 21, no. 8, pp. 21–25.

Cochran-Smith, M. 1991, 'Word processing and writing in elementary classrooms: a critical review of related literature', *Review of Educational Research*, vol. 61, no. 1, pp. 107-55.

Scrimshaw, P. 1993, 'Cooperative writing with computers', in P. Scrimshaw (ed.), *Language, Classrooms and Computers*, Routledge, New York.

Software

WORD PROCESSING

ClarisWorks (Macintosh, Windows 95).

Microsoft Creative Writer (Macintosh, Windows, Macintosh/Windows CD ROM).

Microsoft Word 6.0 (DOS, Macintosh, Windows CD ROM, Windows 95).

My Own Stories (DOS, Macintosh).

Storybook Weaver (DOS, Macintosh, Windows, Apple).

Storybook Weaver Deluxe (Windows/Macintosh CD ROM).

Student Writing Center (Windows, MPC CD ROM).

The Amazing Writing Machine (Macintosh, Windows, Macintosh/MPC CD ROM).

The Children's Writing and Publishing Center (Macintosh, Macintosh CD ROM).

Ultimate Writing and Creativity Center (Macintosh, Windows, Macintosh/Windows CD ROM).

Writer's Toolkit (Macintosh).

CREATING OUTLINES/CONCEPT MAPS

The Amazing Writing Machine (Macintosh, Windows, Macintosh/Windows CD ROM).

DEVELOPING KEYBOARD SKILLS

Kid Keys (DOS, Macintosh).

Mario Teaches Typing (Macintosh, Windows, Macintosh/Windows CD ROM).

Mavis Beacon Teaches Typing (Macintosh, Windows, Macintosh/Windows CD ROM).

Ultra Key (Macintosh, Windows, Macintosh/Windows CD ROM, Windows).

Publishing

Signs, notices, posters, advertisements, newsletters, magazines, newspapers, instruction booklets — few of these everyday texts find a home on library shelves or feature prominently in classroom literacy programs. Yet they are all intended for people to read and they have a significant communicative role in our social, economic and political lives. They also account for a great proportion of the environmental print that children encounter outside the classroom.

Generally these texts are multi-modal; in other words, they combine the elements of written language, images and graphic design to enhance their communicative power. Design as well as content (words and images) is shaped for identifiable audiences and for specific purposes.

The process of creating and publishing such texts puts children in a situation where they are engaged in public writing with a strong sense of their aims and audience. This injects a purposefulness that they often fail to perceive in other forms of writing, and at the same time it allows the teacher to foster a wider range of literacy skills. For example, if time is given to the development of graphic design skills, children can improve the visual presentation of their texts. Visual presentation is important for two reasons: firstly, it helps to arouse interest and attract potential readers; secondly, it helps to convey meaning through the visual organisation of the items which make up the text.

In particular, the role of images in conveying meaning needs serious consideration in both the writing and publishing processes. From an early age children are exposed to texts — notably picture books — which rely heavily on the power of images to support and enhance the meaning of the words. Picture books show how images and words can be combined either to reinforce each other or to add meaning in one element which is not apparent in the other. Furthermore young children use drawing as a form of communication themselves, often relying on pictures to convey messages or moving between drawing and writing as they compose. For them images are an integral part of the writing process, just as they are of the reading process.

It's therefore not surprising that aspects of the writing and publishing processes are often indistinct for young children. They may well decide where on the page to write and what colour pen or pencil to write with at the same time as they decide what to write. They frequently create images and make decisions about layout and design features during the composing process. Older writer/publishers are better able to distinguish between the various processes and techniques involved and can adapt them to different purposes and audiences. For example, they can use images more deliberately to attract and focus the reader's attention or to illustrate particular points.

Opportunities to examine how images and other design features are used in a variety of multi-modal texts can help children to become more effective writers and publishers, as well as more effective readers and more discriminating consumers of information. However, just as they need a teacher's guidance to understand and learn to use the various structures and features of different text types, so too they need explicit instruction to be able to interpret and use images and elements of design to enhance their writing and publishing. Thus, in discussing children's multi-modal texts, it is important to respond to the language of the images as well as the written language, and to comment on design features, such as choice of typeface or use of white space, which may attract readers or enhance the meaning of the text.

The use of computer technology to design and produce multi-modal texts is commonly known as 'desktop publishing'. A wide range of software can serve this purpose, ranging from simple writing programs that allow young children to combine words, pictures and colour, right through to professional packages used for commercial layout and design.

Desktop publishing programs may be used to design page layout on-screen, combine words and graphics, vary fonts and styles of text, arrange text in columns and create borders. The final copy can be printed out on a dot matrix, inkjet or laser printer, in colour or black and white, onto paper, printing masters, cardboard, materials, or even silk screens.

Moving between composing and publishing

Many software programs allow young writers to move easily between creating images, writing text and designing layout. Flexibility to move between these processes and to easily edit images and features of the text are key characteristics of good software, particularly for younger writers. The teacher in the following classroom story selected two programs that allowed some flexibility and were simple enough for the children to use independently as they worked on multi-modal texts.

Classroom story

Kevin was teaching a class of seven- and eight-year-olds and was rather concerned that they lacked interest in editing and publishing their writing. Part of the explanation, he thought, was a perceived lack of audience and therefore a lack of purpose for turning early drafts into published texts. He hoped that if he provided opportunities for the children to present their writing with a more professional looking finish to attract a wider audience, he would be able to inspire them to work through the publishing process with more enthusiasm.

He decided to use two simple writing programs with desktop publishing facilities. The first, called *The Children's Writing and Publishing Center*, gives a choice of three basic formats: either body text with a heading, a report format or a letter format. It also allows graphics to be added to complement the text. The second program, *Once Upon a Time*, encourages children to create a picture before writing; they have the choice of an underwater, dinosaur or forest scene on which to add graphics. The graphics are selected by scrolling through an extensive wordbank, and when a word is selected, it is spoken by the computer before the picture appears. Kevin felt that this program would be particularly suitable for the second language learners in his class, and for some children with special learning needs.

He began by grouping the children according to their language background and giving them a narrative writing task related to other classroom work. As the small groups took turns at the computer, he encouraged them to talk about their story-line in their first language and to write in English. He noticed that the children interacted most effectively when he was not directly involved, with the second language learners alternating between using English and their first language. Consequently, although he did need to be around sometimes to give help with using the software, he made sure that the children had lots of opportunities to discuss their ideas 'in private'.

The small groups regularly conferenced with Kevin on completion of a first draft. On one occasion, however, he sent the children home with printed copies of their first drafts to edit with a pen, as they would handwritten work. This provoked many unfavourable comments: 'It made it messy. . . . It looks like we made lots of mistakes. . . . I didn't want to show my mum.' As a result Kevin planned to conference each group's writing at the computer for a few weeks so that the children could edit directly on the screen. He thought this would help them to view their writing more positively because there would be no evidence of corrections. Nevertheless he planned to demonstrate later on that editing a printed copy is an integral part of the publishing process, so that children could more easily accept editing marks on their own copies.

As the children gained greater competence in using the software, Kevin noticed a corresponding increase in the meaningful use of words such as *delete, change, backspace, shift, save, edit, print* and *publish*. Terminology describing the conventions of writing was also being used appropriately: terms such as *capitals, full stops, commas* and *headings* were discussed, understood and applied.

An early draft of the beginning of one group's narrative using Once Upon A Time.

While he was working with the groups who were using *Once Upon a Time* to create their own books, Kevin made a point of discussing the role and composition of the illustrations. In one session he introduced the notion of connections between words and pictures by having the children examine a range of familiar picture books, including Pat Hutchins' *Rosie's Walk*, Peter Pavey's *Battles in the Bath* and Robert Munsch's *The Paper Bag Princess*. The children were asked to describe the pictures in terms of whether they retold the story, added detail or changed the story in some way. This generated much discussion about what the children would add to their own illustrations, and when the time came for them to use the computer again, they were editing both words and pictures.

When he was working with the groups using *Children's Writing and Publishing Center*, Kevin concentrated on other aspects of the design process. These texts would be published on noticeboards in various locations around the school, such as corridors outside classrooms and foyers in the library and administration section. The groups considered who would be likely to see them, what design features would attract people to stop and read them, and how long they might spend reading. These questions led to discussion about the desirable length of a story and the need for a brief but interesting orientation. The size and style of font was also discussed at some length since it would play an important part in determining readability. Finally groups talked about the use of pictures, both to arouse interest and to enhance the story. Kevin was concerned that the children generally preferred to use graphics provided with the software, even though the choice was fairly limited. He put this down partly to novelty value, but he was none the less concerned that using these limited and at times stereotyped images might stifle the children's creativity. Accordingly he promoted the use of hand-drawn illustrations whenever this suited the purpose or content of the writing.

Trying it out

- Identify writing tasks where the purpose and audience indicate the need for a multi-modal text. Simple examples include banners welcoming visitors to the school or announcing special events, posters or signs identifying places or giving instructions, or procedures and explanations that the school community needs to see. (Note that there are special programs available for producing banners and large posters.)
- Select software to suit the needs of the children and the purpose of the writing. For younger writers in particular, the software should be flexible and simple to use. Moving between words, images and layout should be easy, as should the editing of each element. Beware of programs that only allow you to edit the text.
- Discuss purpose, audience and text type with the children and involve them in some of the decisions.
- Discuss the role of text, images and layout at the planning stage. Sometimes layout decisions have implications for the amount of text that can be fitted on the page; sometimes the use of diagrams may reduce the need for extended text.
- Introduce children to the basic features of the software and provide time for them to explore it and become reasonably confident in using it. More advanced features can be introduced to individuals and small groups on a needs basis.
- Introduce the multi-modal text type with the same care as you would any other text type. Consider modelling, teacher-led joint construction and independent construction in small groups as part of the learning process.
- When you are conferencing children's work, attend to the content of the images as well as the words and discuss key design features.
- Encourage children to add their own illustrations or modify available computer graphics to ensure that the images support the content and fit with the layout.

Desktop publishing with ten- and eleven-year-olds

As children gain more experience with publishing their own texts, they can begin to work on group projects in which each group member is responsible for a specific task, such as illustration or proofreading. Some projects may be large enough to require whole class collaboration. In the world of commercial publishing, many people with different areas of expertise must work together to produce the finished product — whether it be a newspaper, a magazine, a book or an advertising campaign. Some teachers have reproduced this situation in their classrooms. For example, 'Newsdays' became popular a few years ago, not only as a forum for writing and publishing, but also because they gave children opportunities to play the roles of newspaper professionals working towards a deadline.

In the following classroom story the children are engaged in a whole class project to produce a class booklet about the environment.

Classroom story

Each year the senior primary children at Roula's school undertake a substantial unit of work on the environment. 'How can we improve our school environment?' has been a major focus in recent units. One year the children undertook a thorough study of the paper rubbish that the office and classrooms produced. Working from their analysis and their growing understanding of recycling processes, they made some suggestions about the use of paper in the school. A number of changes were agreed, which they communicated through letters to teachers, assembly announcements and posters placed at strategic points around the school.

Another focus of the unit was 'Can we provide natural alternatives to protect and care for our planet?', which involved the children in a series of experiments using natural alternatives to commercially available cleaning products. Subsequently the class published a booklet, 'The Senior School Guide to the Care and Protection of Our Planet', which contained information about the natural alternatives they found useful, ways to use them, and helpful hints of a general nature. It was produced by using scissors and paste to combine the children's handwritten texts, and copies were distributed to families and friends of children in senior primary.

Bicarbonate of Soda

* Here are some ideas for using bicarbonate of soda for cleaning. You can use bicarbonate of soda for cleaning sinks, tiles, toilets, bowls and baths. You can clean these things by adding a little bit of bicarbonate of soda into water. Bicarbonate of soda can get grease stains off.
* You use bicarbonate of soda in clean, cold or hot water and you use a rag to get the stains off.

continued next page. →

continued.

Bicarbonate of Soda

* Year 5 have successfully used bicarbonate of soda as a natural alternative to chemicals.

Contributed by Rebecca Gerards and Darren

a natural alternative

Bicarbonate of Soda

PS If it doesn't work for you, you must have done something wrong because it worked for us.

A sample of the handwritten booklet.

The following year Roula was keen to use the desktop publishing features of her word processing software to improve the quality of the class's publications. She had one computer in her classroom and access to another with a high quality printer in the staffroom. The children had had some experience with word processing but had never undertaken any desktop publishing projects before. So, in consultation with the school's computer coordinator, Roula developed a term-long plan that would involve all the children in some aspect of the computer-based publishing process.

In the 'How can we improve our school environment?' module, children focused their research on the waste products from the canteen and the playground. This was timely as the local council had recently introduced a major recycling system for containers, as well as a 'Use Compost Bins' campaign which provided information, advice and cheap compost bins for all ratepayers. The children developed a slogan for their school-based campaign — *Recycle your food and be a cool dude!* — and set about designing a letterhead.

Children worked in groups of two or three at the two computers, using a variety of graphics programs to design and print out possible letterheads. Roula had prepared them by presenting a wide selection of specimens and discussing the design features, and by demonstrating the basic features of the software as she jointly constructed a letterhead with the whole class.

All versions of the letterhead were displayed, and Roula and the children discussed various appealing features of the designs. Each group then had the opportunity to improve their design (drawing on feedback from the discussion) and to use their letterhead to write to their own families explaining the forthcoming campaign. Finally one design was chosen for external correspondence and for use in a modified form on posters.

Letterhead designs created in small groups.

As their campaign continued, the children (with the principal's approval) sought advice from the local council about beginning a small system to compost fruit and vegetable waste from the staffroom and canteen and the playground rubbish bins. Groups of children were involved in designing posters to be placed around the school. All groups had to use a common template but were free to design the layout of the information or instructions as they chose. Issues of white space and size of lettering were raised in a whole class discussion, during which the children viewed and commented on a range of appealing posters they had brought in. The issue of using computer-based graphics arose later when one group found some 'almost suitable' images in one of the school's clip art collections.

By the time this four-week module came to an end, all children had worked in groups at the computers, designing, refining and printing letterheads, letters and posters.

In the final module, 'Can we provide natural alternatives to protect and care for our planet?', Roula used a different approach for the publishing process. She divided the class into teams consisting of reporters, editors, artists and layout designers, with two children nominated as managing editors to oversee the whole production. She decided on the membership of groups, taking into account the children's varying expertise, needs and interests. A time-line was developed in a whole class discussion to ensure that the booklet would be ready for distribution at the end of five weeks.

	WEEK 1	**WEEK 2**	**WEEK 3**	**WEEK 4**	**WEEK 5**
Reporters	Experiment with substances to be described in articles.	Continue experiments.	Present first drafts of articles to editors.	Conference articles with editors.	Produce final drafts.
Editors	Become familiar with experi-ments being conducted.	Talk with reporters about types of articles needed.	Read first drafts of articles; consult with artists.	Conference articles with reporters.	Ensure that all articles are complete.
Artists	Small group lesson on photography; time to practise with a roll of film.	Photograph experiments.	Look for suitable graphics in the school's clip art collections.	Consult with layout designers and decide on graphics.	Provide final graphics and photographs to layout designers.
Layout Designers	Become familiar with necessary features of the software.	Design page layouts to discuss with editorial team.	Experiment with title, contents and acknowledge-ments pages.	Experiment with formatting for articles; discuss choice of graphics with artists.	Finalise layout of articles, graphics and photographs.

Time-line for the production process.

Reporters worked in pairs, each pair being responsible for the production of an article about one of a number of substances (cream of tartar, lemon, vinegar, pure soap and bicarbonate of soda) which were the subject of a set of experiments during the first two weeks of the module. One pair was responsible for a page on the use of natural products to control pests. All the reporters had to compose their articles on a word processor and present them to their editors by the end of Week 3.

Editors had to work with the reporters to edit, refine and proofread the articles. They also had to confer with the artists about access to suitable photographs and computer-based or hand-drawn graphics. This process had to be completed by the middle of Week 4.

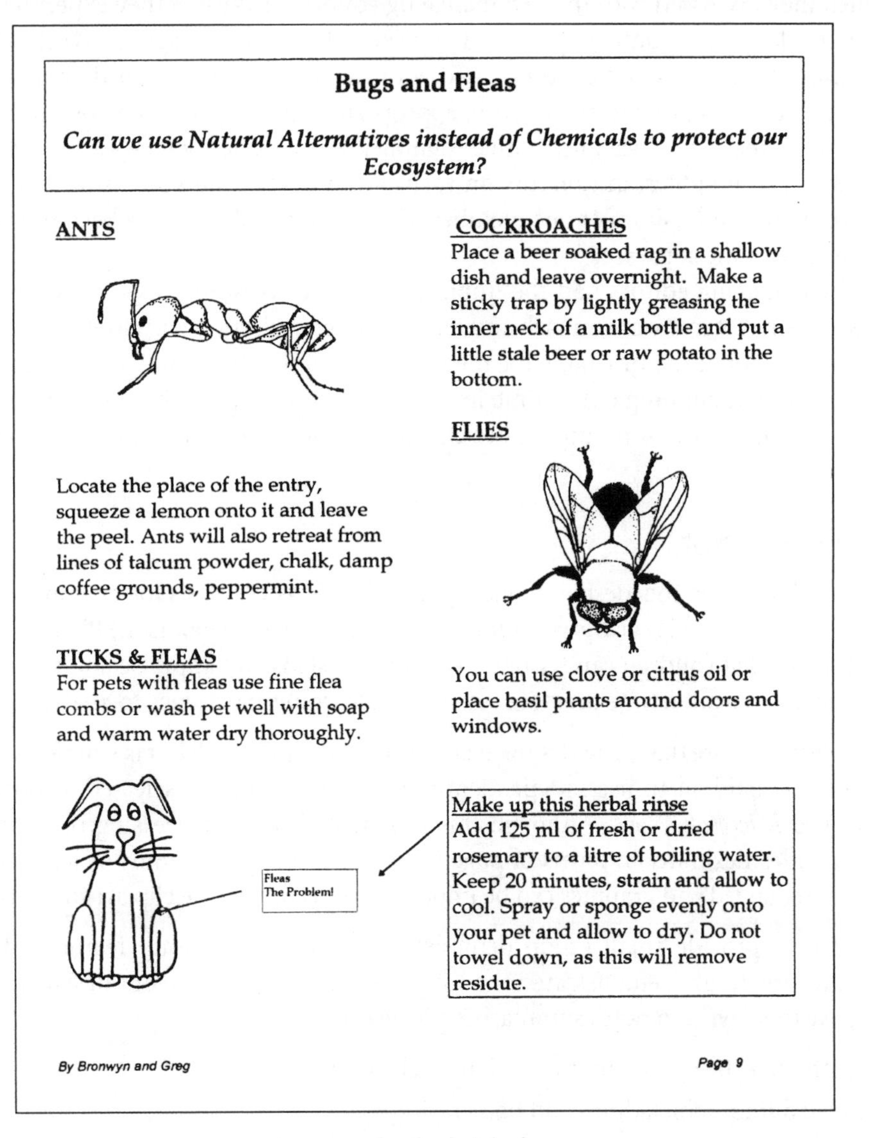

Bugs and Fleas

Can we use Natural Alternatives instead of Chemicals to protect our Ecosystem?

ANTS

Locate the place of the entry, squeeze a lemon onto it and leave the peel. Ants will also retreat from lines of talcum powder, chalk, damp coffee grounds, peppermint.

TICKS & FLEAS
For pets with fleas use fine flea combs or wash pet well with soap and warm water dry thoroughly.

Fleas
The Problem!

COCKROACHES
Place a beer soaked rag in a shallow dish and leave overnight. Make a sticky trap by lightly greasing the inner neck of a milk bottle and put a little stale beer or raw potato in the bottom.

FLIES

You can use clove or citrus oil or place basil plants around doors and windows.

Make up this herbal rinse
Add 125 ml of fresh or dried rosemary to a litre of boiling water. Keep 20 minutes, strain and allow to cool. Spray or sponge evenly onto your pet and allow to dry. Do not towel down, as this will remove residue.

By Bronwyn and Greg

Page 9

An example of a finished page.

Artists were responsible for taking photographs of the various substances and experiments during Weeks 1 and 2. They had a small group lesson from two senior high school students with photographic expertise and were given one roll of film to practise with. They also had to search the school's clip art collections for graphics that might be used in the booklet. Decisions about graphics had to be finalised in consultation with the layout team by the end of Week 4.

Layout designers were initially responsible for becoming familiar with the features and functions of the software that they would need to use later on. Roula took time to give this group a demonstration of a range of the features and some summary notes of the demonstration. During Week 2 they designed a series of page layouts which they discussed with the two managing editors. In Week 3 they experimented with a title page, a contents page and an acknowledgements page. In Week 4 they finalised these pages and experimented with the draft articles from the reporters, checking their length and considering appropriate type sizes and the positioning of graphics. Week 5 was occupied with designing the final page layout — arranging the written text, graphics and photos on each of the pages. The success of this team rested on the enthusiasm of one member who spent lots of free time becoming very familiar with the software.

The managing editors had the important role of overseeing the whole project, checking that teams were on task and on time. In consultation with Roula, they had overall control of the timetable for the use of the computers, and when the project appeared to be running out of time in Week 4, they arranged with another teacher to have access to the computer in her classroom before and after school and during lunch.

Trying it out

➤ Consider using the 'design, make, appraise' cycle as the basis for creating multimodal texts. (This cycle is common to most Technology syllabuses.) Plan for extra time so that children can try out a variety of designs and appraise and refine the results. Too often time pressure restricts the learning experience to 'making' only.

➤ Select software that provides the features needed for the task but is simple enough for the children to use independently. Roula, for example, selected a program called *Microsoft Word*. Although this is actually a word processing program, it provides flexibility in terms of page layout — blocks or columns of text can be interchanged and graphics can be imported from compatible clip art software.

➤ Plan to provide small group demonstrations of the necessary features of the software. Roula demonstrated the software to her group of layout designers and gave them written notes summarising its features.

➤ Introduce the key features of design and layout:

– headlines, subheadings and body text

– visual appeal

- balance
- white space
- basic typography
- content-related graphics.

McCain (1992) is a useful guide here.

- Provide opportunities for children to examine a variety of publications and compare the various design features.
- Allow ample time for children to experiment with layout. In terms of the final publication, this is as important as the time provided for editing text.
- Provide opportunities for children to learn how to use the necessary technologies. Roula arranged for two high school students to teach the artists about photography and allocated one roll of film for practice shots.
- Involve children in planning a time-frame for the publication process and listing the responsibilities of each group. They will feel greater ownership of a plan they have helped to develop themselves.
- Ensure access to a good quality printer for printing the final copy. If the school does not have a suitable printer, then ask families. Parents may have access to a good printer at work, if not at home.

Issues to consider when planning to enhance the publishing process

What is the difference between word processing and desktop publishing?

Essentially, the emphasis in word processing is on composing, editing and proofreading text — on the manipulation of words to create effective messages — while the emphasis in desktop publishing is on the manipulation of text and graphics as design elements. However, the distinction is blurred in common usage, and to some extent that reflects the increasing sophistication of word processing software.

Word processing programs are now available with a variety of different features. Basic features include the ability to enter, edit, save and print text. However, most programs also allow some basic formatting in relation to type area, font style and size and text layout, while more recent programs may offer quite sophisticated formatting options. Programs designed for young children may allow the use of large or coloured print and 'spoken' output of composed text. Programs for older writers may include spell checkers, thesauruses, grammar checkers, outliners and formatting options such as columns and tables. Some programs can produce or include graphics, and some allow the use of non-English characters. A text created on a word processing program can be read from the screen, printed or imported into a desktop publishing program.

The most advanced desktop publishing programs can now produce work of professional standard (like this book) because they offer facilities for much more delicate design adjustments than do word processing programs. For example, the spacing between individual letters and words can be varied to very fine tolerances. However, many of these facilities assume a level of expertise which is seldom found in the primary school and is certainly not required. Moreover most dedicated desktop publishing programs do not provide a very friendly environment for creating and editing text. And since most recent word processing software includes the basics of desktop publishing software, it is generally suitable for classroom applications. Thus Roula chose a sophisticated word processing program for designing the class booklet. Similarly the software programs that Kevin selected to use with his class were writing programs that incorporated simple formatting features and allowed the inclusion of graphics.

Some desktop publishing software for children is designed for specific purposes, such as creating banners, greeting cards, calendars, time-lines, big books, oversize posters, newsletters and newspapers. Decisions about what type of program is most appropriate should be based on the needs of the children who will be using it and the desired outcomes.

Common features of software that can be used for desktop publishing tasks include:

- availability of a variety of fonts and styles of text (e.g. italic, bold)
- ability to mix text and graphics
- ability to cut and paste, move and modify elements of the design
- option to import graphics and text from other programs, such as clip art collections
- facility to format text in tables, columns and blocks and wrap it around graphics.

These features are not restricted to desktop publishing programs; many paint/draw and word processing programs include them.

How does access to graphics affect the writing and publishing processes?

When children are composing, they frequently move between drawing and writing. Young children may in fact rely almost solely on drawing to record their ideas, using talk rather than written text to share these ideas with others, while older children are generally more able to record their ideas directly in text form (Blackstock & Miller 1992). However, the relationship between text and drawing varies with individual children, with some continually moving between the two, others needing to complete a drawing before they feel ready to write about it, and others relying completely on text.

The relationship between talking, drawing and writing needs to be borne in mind when you are selecting and using software to aid the writing process, particularly in relation to programs which incorporate ready-made graphics. Often children prefer to use one of these rather than adding their own hand-drawn illustrations — even if none of the graphics available match their writing. Kevin found this to be the case in his classroom. You need to take care that hand-drawn illustrations are valued as highly as computer-generated pictures, so that children feel free to write on the topic of their choice rather than being constrained by the limitations of the software.

Children should also be able to modify ready-made graphics to match their own experience or requirements more closely. Some word processing programs include basic drawing tools which allow graphics to be embellished or resized. Children writing within a paint/draw program can use the tools provided to adapt graphics to their own text. Alternatively they may need to modify a graphic within a paint/draw program and then copy and paste it into their writing program.

Given the importance of drawing as part of the composing process, especially for young children, you should be aware that straight word processing programs may not offer the flexibility of moving between graphics and text. The facility to incorporate individualised graphics may be an important factor when you are selecting software for use with young children.

Even with older children, differences in learning styles may mean that some children prefer to draw a picture first, while others prefer to write first. Setting up a word processing program and a paint/draw program simultaneously will allow spatial learners and verbal learners to work in the modality that best matches their learning style (Reissman 1993). Another advantage of this approach is that using the two types of software together helps to reinforce the connection between words and images.

How can desktop publishing be integrated with English and other curriculum areas?

So often the computer is seen as a way of producing neater work rather than a powerful means of learning new skills and processes. As children use computers to publish their work, they have greater control over many aspects of the design process than ever before. However, they need to understand some of the principles of graphic design so that they can use this tool to enhance the communicative power of their messages. They need time to play with, learn about, use and reflect upon design elements. Opportunities for such learning occur in a range of situations across grades and curriculum tasks. For example:

- 4–5-year-olds playing with a range of fonts and font sizes as they print out their names for the 'Welcome' message on the classroom door (*Which fonts are more readable . . . from a distance . . . up close? What size does the font need to be to readable from the verandah? Which font size will allow Elizabeth's name to fit in a particular space?*)

- 6–7-year-olds playing with a range of graphics from a clip art collection to decide which, if any, enhance their message about placing litter in the bins provided, or knocking before entering the staffroom
- 8–9-year-olds playing with the layout of their information report on mini-beasts (placement of titles, text and images)
- 10–11-year-olds playing with the design of a school magazine in terms of front and internal page design, section design, use of borders, columns, etc.

For further reading, viewing or playing

Books and articles

Blackstock, J. & Miller, L. 1992, 'The impact of new information technology on young children's symbol-weaving efforts', *Computers in Education*, vol. 18, nos 1–3, pp. 209–21.

McCain, T. D. E. 1992, *Designing for Communication: The Key to Successful Desktop Publishing*, International Society for Technology in Education, Eugene, Oregon.

Reissman, R. 1993, 'Software duos: multiple entry points for learning', *The Computing Teacher*, vol. 21, no. 3, p. 17.

Software

Big Book Maker (Apple II, Macintosh).

ClarisWorks (Macintosh, Windows, Windows 95).

Imagination Express (Macintosh/Windows CD ROM).

Microsoft Creative Writer (Macintosh, Windows, Macintosh/Windows CD ROM).

Microsoft Word (DOS, Macintosh, Windows, Macintosh/Windows CD ROM, Windows 95).

My Own Stories (DOS, Macintosh).

Once Upon a Time (Apple II, DOS, Macintosh).

Storybook Weaver Deluxe (Macintosh/Windows CD ROM).

Student Writing Center (Macintosh, Windows, Macintosh/Windows CD ROM).

The Children's Writing and Publishing Center (Apple II, DOS, Windows).

The Print Shop Deluxe (DOS, Macintosh, Windows).

WordPerfect (DOS, Windows).

SECTION THREE

Using Electronic Texts

Outside school, electronic texts can be found on screens at automatic teller machines or at information consoles in retail stores and museums. In homes they are most commonly encountered in video games or as CD ROM-based encyclopedias on the family personal computer. Television shows could also be considered as electronic texts, but the extra dimensions of popular culture and mass broadcasting mean that they are more often grouped under the heading of media texts.

Electronic texts come in many forms. They may be published to screen, disk or CD ROM, or reside in networks to be accessed by subscribers. They may be:

- replicas of paper-based texts — in this form the computer may function as little more than a page-turner, or there may be a sophisticated system for searching
- databases which store information about a number of items or people in a systematic manner — unlike their print-based counterparts, these electronic collections can be easily updated, reorganised and searched in a variety of ways
- hypertexts — a term that refers to *non-sequential* text, chunks or screens of which can be linked in several ways. Hypertexts tend to be factual texts where users can travel through a collection of information, beginning and ending in different places and travelling in different directions. Choose your own adventure stories are somewhat similar in that readers have a choice of pathways, but the very essence of narrative moves the reader along a path to a resolution, and in that sense they are still sequential.

Electronic texts may be purely text-based or designed to exploit the power of technology by combining words, images and sounds. In this latter form they are often referred to as 'multimedia'. The advent of CD ROM technologies has allowed multimedia to become universal on most types of recent personal computers.

Just as different genres of written text suit different purposes and audiences, so too do different media and forms of texts. For example, paper-based prose is ideal for presenting arguments or developing complex ideas, paperbacks are ideal for recreational reading, and electronic texts offer powerful ways of working with factual information.

All types of electronic texts, whether they appear to replicate their paper-based equivalents or exploit unique features of the electronic media, require literacy skills additional to or different from those developed in a paper-based environment. Using electronic texts involves a change to scrolling screens (which are usually wider and less deep than book pages) and the loss of some physical cues to identify one's place in the text (e.g. position on page, page number and size of book). Traditional processes of locating specific information, such as using contents pages, indexes and headings and then skim-reading, are replaced by a variety of new processes. These include free text searching for matching characters, words or groups of words, searching documents or parts of documents by keywords, or creating complex searches using connectors such as 'and', 'or' and 'not'. All of these changes impose different literacy demands.

Electronic texts need to be introduced to children with the same degree of care as their paper-based counterparts. The organisation of an electronic text and the conventions used within it need to be made explicit, as is commonly done with children's study of various genres, such as information reports and explanations. Children need time to browse, explore, ask and answer questions, see models and discuss conventions. They also need to be supported as they write their own electronic texts. In most cases they will need to be prepared for the content, structures and functions of the text, as well as for the processes required to operate the technology (hardware and software).

The rest of this chapter explores two types of electronic text, databases and hypertexts. Multimedia texts, combining images, sounds and written texts, are explored in Chapter 8.

Exploring databases in middle primary

Databases are collections of factual information made up of a number of entries or records that share a consistent structure. Paper-based versions include telephone books, street directories and dictionaries. In a telephone book, for example, the information provided for each subscriber includes surname or business name, initials of first names, street address, suburb and telephone number. All entries follow the same order, and each segment of information obeys consistent rules or conventions. Thus all suburbs have a consistent abbreviated form, phone numbers do not include area codes, and initials do not have full stops after them. Electronic databases have consistent entries and conventions too.

Paper-based databases have a fixed order: for instance, telephone books are sorted alphabetically by surname of subscriber, and so the only way we can find a number is through the correct surname. However, electronic databases have more flexible characteristics which present different literacy demands. They can be sorted by different fields (e.g. surname, suburb, postcode or telephone number) and by different criteria (e.g. numerical order, ascending or descending, or alphabetical order, 'a' to 'z' or 'z' to 'a'). In some cases two or three layers of sorting can occur (e.g. by postcode, then suburb, then surname).

In addition, electronic databases offer a wider range of strategies for finding specific bits of information. Users can sort by a particular criterion and then browse that part of the collection to locate the bit of information they want; they can identify a piece of text (e.g. letters, words or phrases) to be matched; they can specify a criterion to search the collection (e.g. *SUBURB begins with SYD*); or they can combine a number of criteria using the connectors 'and', 'or' and 'not' (e.g. *SUBURB is the same as CRONULLA and SURNAME is the same as SMITH*).

Children can make or use a database of information on almost any topic they are investigating, such as homes, pets, plants in the school garden or books in the classroom library. The range of commercially published databases for older children covers such topics as the convicts of the First Fleet, the solar system, bushrangers, famous Australians and members of Parliament.

Reasons commonly given for using electronic databases in the classroom include the following:

- They offer opportunities for a different form of publishing. For example, children's research on endangered species of native animals could be published in the form of an electronic database rather than as information reports on posters.
- As children design and build a database, the need to sort, organise, group and label different types of information extends their conceptual development within the topic. For example, if they are building a database on their pets, they need to identify a limited number of labels to describe the variety of foods the pets eat — a process of categorisation which involves much discussion and requires an understanding of the purpose of the database.
- Electronic databases give children access to different sources and types of information when they are researching topics. Besides consulting experts and the commonly used paper-based texts in the school library, they can search databases and electronic multimedia texts.
- Electronic databases also provide tools which make it easier for children to detect similarities and differences, or trends and patterns, within the data collected. For example, using a database like *The First Fleet*, they can build tables and graphs to help them identify the most common crime, the different ages of the convicts, or the relationship between crime and original sentence (some sentences were commuted to transportation).

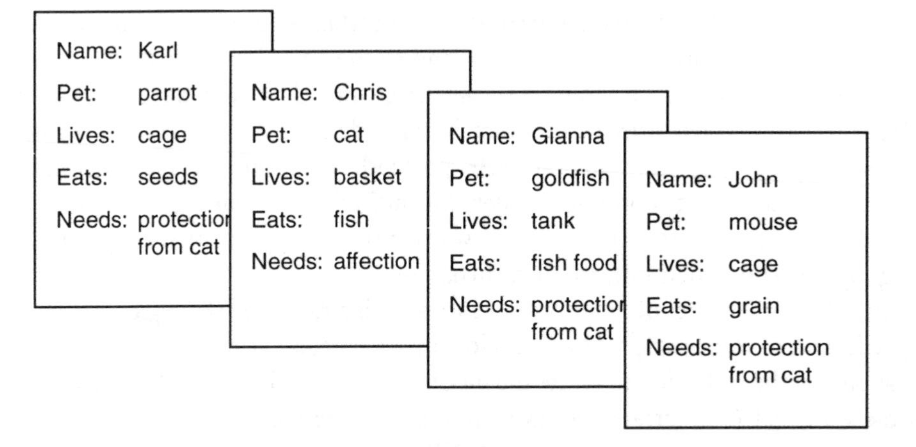

A card representation of part of an electronic database developed during a study of pet care. Each record has the same five fields.

A common feature of database software available in classrooms is the facility to switch the display between record and table layout. In record mode just one record fills the screen, whereas in table mode each record appears as a row of the table and each column is one of the fields. The table can be sorted by row or by column, which facilitates the identification of trends and patterns.

NAME	PET	LIVES	EATS	NEEDS
Gianna	goldfish	tank	fish food	protection from cat
Karl	parrot	cage	seeds	protection from cat
John	mouse	cage	grain	protection from cat
Chris	cat	basket	fish	affection
Greg	dog	yard	meat	affection & exercise
Christine	bird	cage	seeds	protection from cat
Jenni	cat	basket	cat food	affection

Example of a table layout within a database program.

While these facilities increase the power and flexibility of the electronic database, they also demand a new set of 'reading' skills if the collection is to be used effectively. Selecting the fields to be displayed, organising columns and sorting fields are only some of the skills required. For example, let's imagine some children using the 'Pets' table shown above to answer the question, 'Do animals that need protection from cats live in special places?' They would first have to move the NEEDS column next to the LIVES column and then sort the NEEDS column so that all the pets needing protection are grouped together. These processes need to be explained, modelled and scaffolded during reading activities, just as the processes of using contents pages and indexes are. They are all part of teaching children to read texts.

Classroom story

The nine- and ten-year-olds in Christine's class came from a wide range of language backgrounds — ten of them were Phase 2 ESL learners. They had been using computers for a number of years and had two in their classroom. Because of Christine's focus on literacy, she had put one of the computers in the writing centre and the other in the reading corner. The children were studying the solar system during Term 3, and so there were many resources in both areas directly related to the topic. Indeed, apart from the computers, both areas were fairly typical of those found in many classrooms.

The writing centre had some tables and chairs and lots of different types of paper, together with pens and cards, and some books and posters to stimulate writing ideas. The centre's focus at this time was on the writing of information reports. The computer was equipped with writing and publishing software, and the children each had two disks for saving their written texts. One was a working disk, holding all their work in progress, while the other held the texts they wanted to keep.

The computers were used in free time for writing activities. There was a wall chart for children to record each turn they had, and class rules had been established to settle who had a turn when several pairs or individuals wanted access at the same time. The computers were also used for teacher-directed tasks. For example, when groups of children had researched information on selected planets, they presented their findings in the form of a record card which they added to a class database called 'Celestial Bodies'.

Celestial Bodies

Name:
Named after:
Dist. Sun (mill. kms):
Diameter (kms):
Length of year (days):
Length of day (hours):
Moons:
Description:

Interesting things:

Authors:
Sources of information:

Record card structure in the 'Celestial Bodies' database.

The children used the computers to write information reports on their selected planets as well. In groups of two or three, they came prepared with an organised list of points they wanted to cover in their report (these points were based on their database record). Then they cooperatively composed their text sitting around the screen.

The reading corner had quite a number of book and display shelves, with lots of commercially published and school published books and magazines. There was also a disk-based collection of children's narratives and factual texts. Database programs available included the commercially published *Solar System* and the class published 'Celestial Bodies'.

To further develop their reading of the databases, Christine organised the children in pairs to make up questions about the information held in them. The questions were recorded on cards for a question box, but before children could add a question to the box they had to prepare a model answer, which was checked by another class member. (Christine had previously discussed and demonstrated various structures and types of questions with the whole class.) During reading sessions and free time children could search the databases or other texts to answer any of the questions they chose. This proved to be a very popular task.

One pair of emerging readers selected the same question ('How many moons does Saturn have?') on three separate occasions, and each time they were very proud that they could find the answer. The first time they searched on 'moons', and since this was a field name which appeared on every record, it meant flipping through all of the records. The second time they refined their searching strategy by deciding (after much discussion) to search on 'Saturn'. Christine then suggested they sort through the question box to find other 'How many' questions and look for answers to these. When they attempted the first one ('How many moons does Mercury have?'), they reverted to searching on 'moons'. About half way through their scanning of all the records, the following conversation took place:

RENNIE: This is taking too long! We need to go straight to Mercury.
MAYA: But we're almost there! (*She continues to flip through the records*)
RENNIE: No! Go back and FIND Mercury — that's a better way!
MAYA: Look . . . here it is . . . there are no moons.

After successfully finding answers to three more 'How many' questions, the children came to this one: 'How many planets in our solar system have moons?' Again they went back to the 'FIND moons' strategy and were soon flipping through all the records counting those with moons. During a later discussion Christine demonstrated how to sort the whole collection on the 'moons' field, so that counting would be easier. In a subsequent session the two children (who were now fascinated by moons) wrote two new questions: 'Which planet has the most moons?' and 'Which planets have one moon like earth?' In developing their model answers, they used the 'SORT numerically' facility and quickly flipped through to the appropriate place in the collection.

Christine was surprised at the amount of discussion about ways of finding answers which was generated at both whole class and small group levels. In response, she introduced to the morning's reading session a short period during which children could share their strategies for finding answers to different types of questions.

Trying it out

- Allow yourself time to become familiar with the database software you will be using. Use a range of commercial databases as well. School librarians are usually great resources for database work!
- Carefully select your topic and purpose for using an electronic database. Databases suit topics where children need to find out or report on a range of examples (e.g. 'Our Homes', 'Our Pets', 'People Who Help Us', 'Early Australian Explorers', 'Mammals' or 'Endangered Species'). Remember that most electronic databases handle words, phrases, lists and numbers more easily than long segments of prose. Since the information in most collections is accordingly brief, always present other sources of information alongside a database.
- Give children opportunities to use existing collections before they build their own. (Christine provided access to commercial examples for her class.) Children also need to see simple models of databases that reflect the essential features they will be expected to create, such as field names, use of common measures (e.g. length in cms), and common labels (e.g. 'boy'/'girl' only for gender, rather than a mixture of 'boy'/'girl', 'boys'/'girls', 'male'/'female' and 'm'/'f').
- Build extra time into your unit of work for teaching the children how to use the software and for familiarising them with database structure and conventions. Both aspects of using an electronic database need to be made explicit, and this can be done through demonstrations of how to operate the software, making lists of conventions and creating a card-based model of the collection.
- Make printouts of individual records and tables which children can use as concrete representations of the screen images to:
  - investigate how the information is structured within the collection
  - become familiar with the language conventions used
  - work through the processes of sorting, grouping and labelling, and finding and searching.

Using hypertext to organise information

Many electronic texts have structures similar to their paper-based counterparts. However, hypertext (i.e. non-sequential text in which screenfuls of information can be linked together in various ways) goes well beyond any paper-based equivalent. It is an ideal environment for composing and reading factual texts because it is not constrained by a linear structure. In paper-based texts authors have to use a range of devices, such as footnotes, appendices, glossaries, indexes and reference lists, to signal indirect links to other documents, ideas or ways of thinking. Hypertext can make these links directly. For example, if this was a hypertext, readers unfamiliar with the hypertext concept could choose to 'click on' a button that would lead them to a further explanation or an example, as shown in the diagram below.

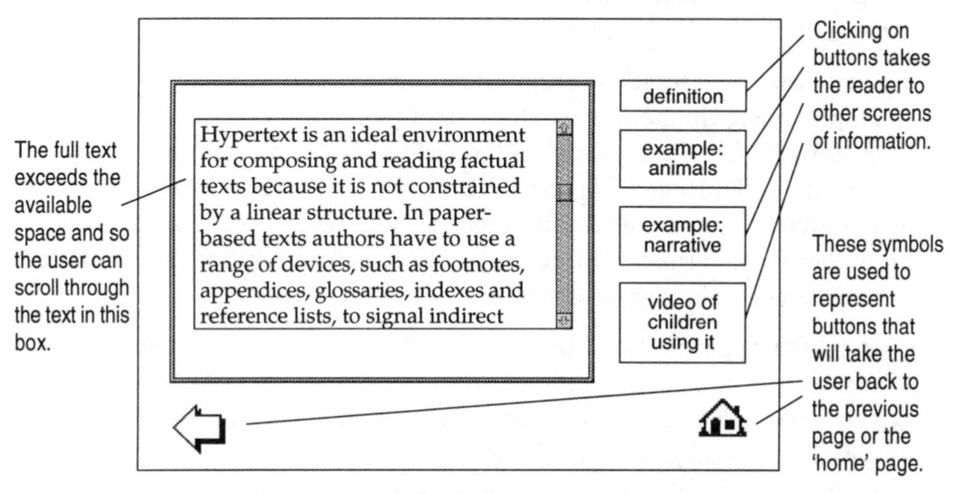

An example of a hypertext screen.

Authors of hypertext can create a number of links between chunks of text and a variety of other resources. The networks formed by the links vary in complexity and structure. They can be linear, hierarchical, web-like or any combination of these. The

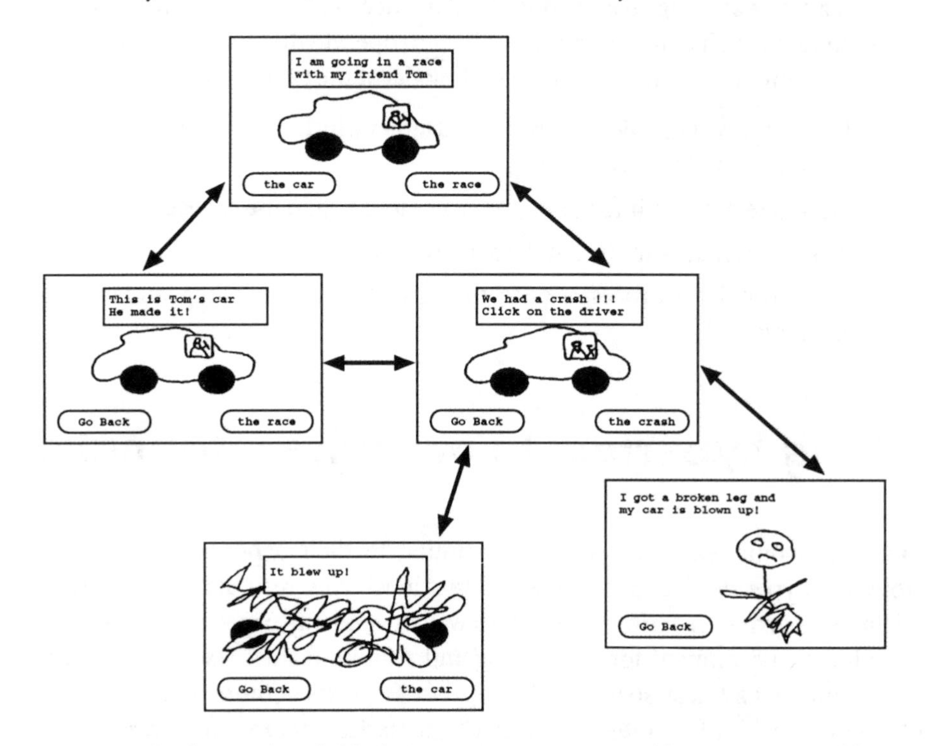

An example of a simple web-like hypertext narrative created by two six-year-olds.

lack of linearity in the overall structure and the presence of linking 'buttons' encourages readers to choose their own pathway through the information.

Many hypertext authoring programs exist, and in some ways they resemble word processors because users can type in and edit text. The most important difference is that users can also create links between the various chunks of text that they write. Each program has its own language to describe its operating system: *Hypercard*, for instance, uses the analogy of stacks, cards, buttons and links. Stacks are collections of cards linked together with buttons that you can click on with your mouse to travel to another card. Cards with multiple links have multiple buttons. In the narrative example on the previous page, the buttons have labels giving information to help the reader decide where to go next.

Classroom story

In Term 3, Ann's class of eleven- and twelve-year-olds were involved in an exciting and topical unit of work, based on the Society and its Environment curriculum. Their focus question was 'How do people shape their future?', and it provided many opportunities for talking, listening, reading and writing. Ann was keen to encourage the children to use and create electronic texts within the unit, as well as paper-based ones.

The children began researching their own family and cultural backgrounds by interviewing members of their families. Ann helped them to use this information to construct family trees and draft brief family histories. She also gave them lots of opportunities to share and discuss their findings in small groups and as a whole class.

The children each made a miniature flag to symbolise their family's country of origin, and these were fixed to a large map of the world to provide a visual representation of the diversity in cultural backgrounds. Then the numbers from each country were keyed into a graphing program, displayed in a bar graph and printed. This led to an interesting discussion about the various cultural backgrounds represented and the patterns of immigration that had emerged over the last few decades.

The next task was for each child to write a factual text about his or her family background. As part of the writing process, children were involved in library research to find out as much as they could about the countries and regions in which their families had originated. Some of this research was done using electronic texts stored on CD ROM in the library.

The children had used *Hypercard* before and were familiar with the nature of the program and the features of the software. Ann briefly reviewed these with the whole class, using hypertexts they had previously made. Then, as the children began to gather information about their countries, she helped them to organise their findings. A common set of headings was selected for the country cards and a similar set for the regional cards. The children typed the information they had gathered onto cards within the *Hypercard* program. Since they still had access to all the editing facilities of a word processor, they were easily able to add new information as they did further research. Equally they could rearrange sections of text within a card to improve its overall organisation.

Ann also initiated a class discussion about a common structure for the *Hypercard* stack. After much debate, the class decided to use a map of the world as the main card. It would lead to information on individual countries and thence to family information. Another possibility for the main card had been a class photo, with family information leading to country information, but the class had reluctantly abandoned this idea when they found that the school did not have the scanning equipment required.

The map of the world dominated the main page.

The map of the world and maps of individual countries were electronically cut and pasted from the school's clip art collection and CD ROM-based encyclopedias. On the world map the children positioned a button to mark each family's country of origin. These buttons linked the main card to one or more cards of information about the selected country. Each of these cards was in turn linked by buttons to other cards containing the children's factual texts about their family backgrounds. Where two or more families originated in one country, that country's information card had several buttons.

There were a number of children whose family histories were located entirely in Australia. They included Aboriginal children and those who could not trace a family history beyond Australia. These children decided to create a card with a map of Australia showing state boundaries and place their buttons near the region where their ancestors or great-grandparents had lived. The buttons were linked to cards

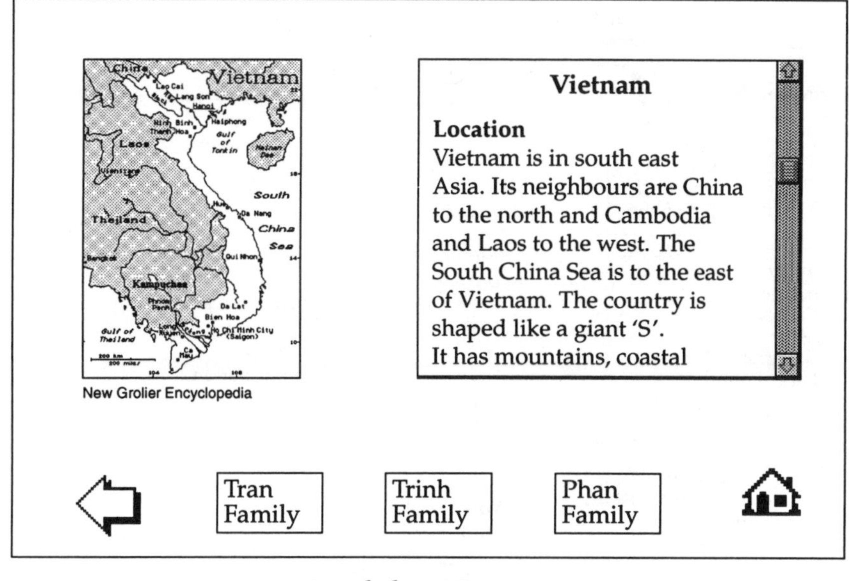

A card about Vietnam.

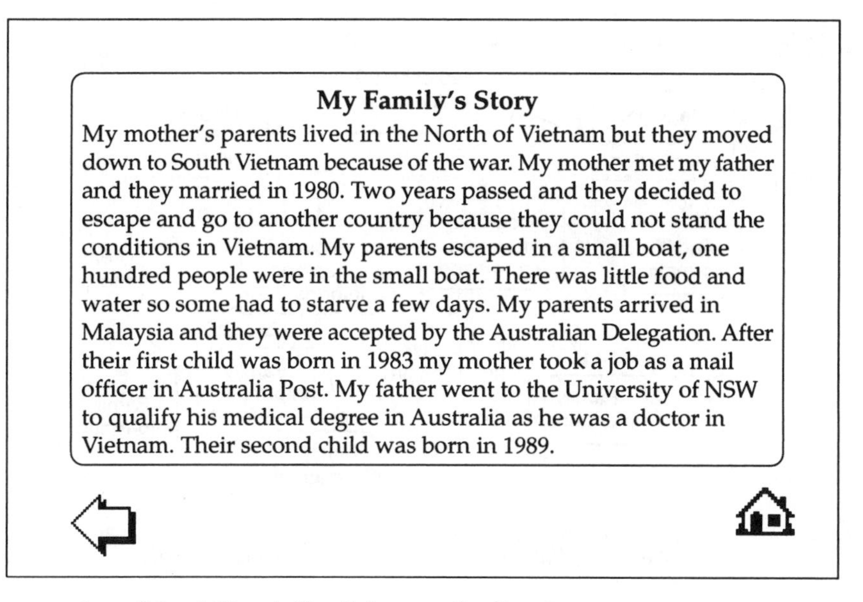

One of the children's 'family' screens leading from a country screen.

containing information about each particular region. This added a layer of complexity to the structure of the hypertext, and so Ann had a group of children draw a diagram of the cards and links, which was used as a reference when children were creating and refining links (see overleaf). Towards the end of the work, regional maps of the Middle East and Indo-China were added as well to reduce the crowding of buttons on the main world map.

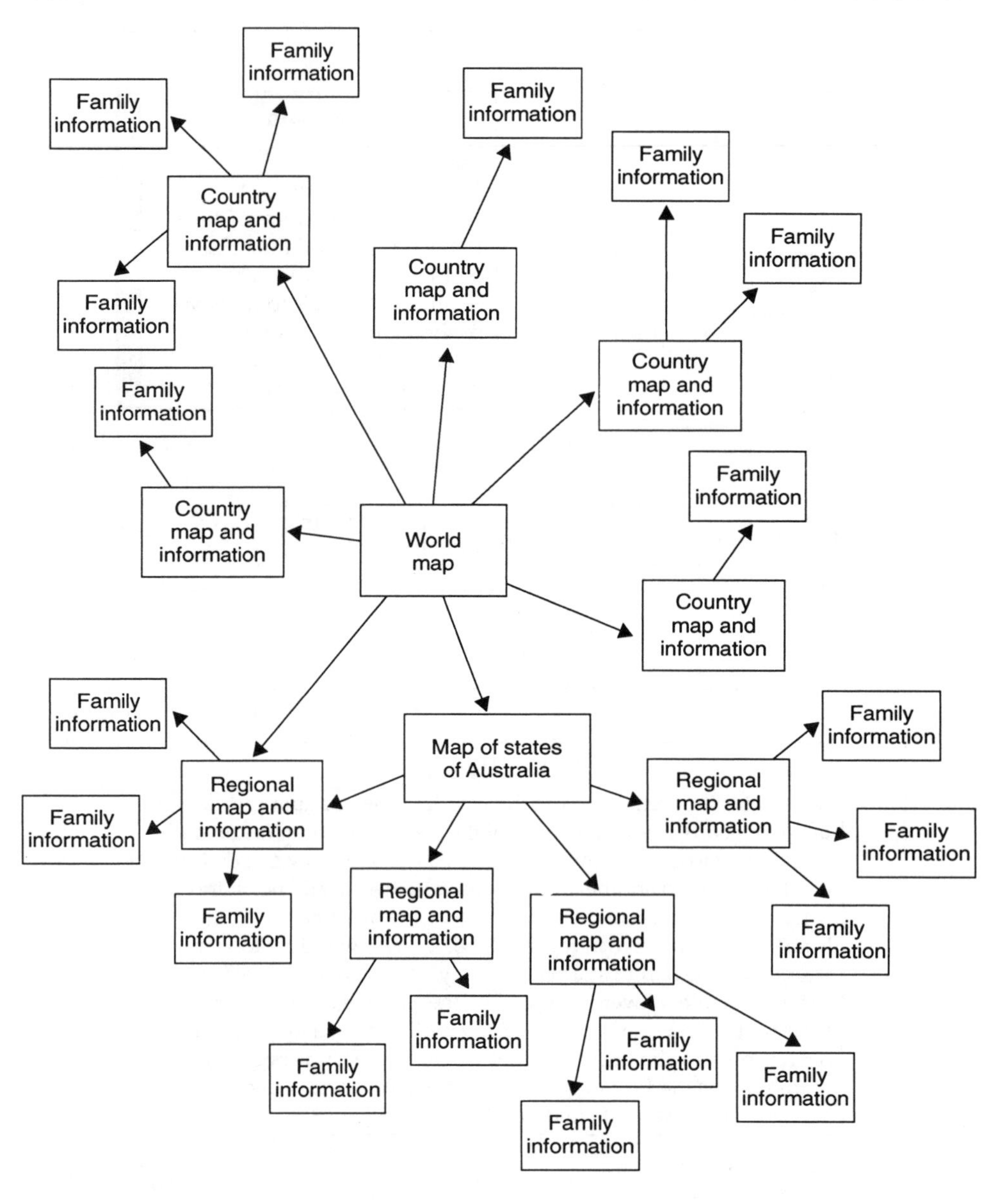

A drawing of the original structure of the stack of cards.

Children continued working on their own parts of the text during timetabled language blocks over several weeks. As all the country and family information had to be typed into the one hypertext, Ann developed a roster system which allowed all children regular access to the program. When everything was completed, a group of children made a presentation at the school assembly and invited children in other classes to visit the computer in the library, which now held a copy of the hypertext. In addition, families were invited to the school to see their children's work as part of the culminating activities of the unit.

Trying it out

- Allow yourself time to use a range of hypertexts before using any in the classroom.
- Locate appropriate resources (people, 'how to' books, etc.) to help you develop a simple hypertext yourself. It's easier than you think!
- Select the unit of work in which you would like to incorporate the use of hypertext. Develop a time-line that allows a long enough period for children to become familiar with the topic and the software before they need to begin writing.
- Consider using the same teaching cycle as you use when teaching a new genre. Aim to reach the joint construction stage on your first attempt. Children can write sections of the text independently, but overall this initial hypertext will be a teacher-directed joint construction.
- Introduce children to the notion of hypertext through demonstrations and structured experiences with ready-made hypertexts supplied with the software. Most commercially produced hypertexts are too complex to be good models for beginning authors — though it is important to make children aware that almost all electronic factual texts (e.g. encyclopedias, atlases and almanacs) are hypertexts.
- Provide opportunities for children to explore a range of hypertext stacks. A variety of simple and commercial texts could be made available for them to read during free time, silent reading and other set reading sessions.
- Create a card and string model of one of the hypertexts and discuss the concepts of stacks, cards, buttons and links (or whatever terminology your hypertext software uses). Children need an overview of the structure of the text so that they know which cards are linked to each other.
- Demonstrate the key processes: i.e. creating a new card, adding text, making buttons and making links. Use small group and individual mini-lessons to teach other features as needed.
- Tell children about the research task that will eventually lead to the development of a hypertext. Encourage them to think about the information they are collecting in terms of cards, chunks or screenfuls of information. Initially restrict information to text and simple graphics (i.e. ones that can be drawn with the mouse, pasted in from clip art collections, or scanned in — if the school has a scanner).
- Have regular group meetings about the nature and structure of the text as children collect information and draft their cards. Create a card and string model and discuss possible starting points and links.
- Organise children to work in groups to create cards, buttons and links.
- Allow time for children to use their hypertext and share it with others. In using it they are quite likely to find missing or inappropriate links, and audience response is a key factor in the revision process.

Issues to consider when planning to use electronic texts

What are the additional literacies of electronic texts?

USING ELECTRONIC TEXTS

Using the software and hardware. Children need to know how to use the computer and load and use the software, how to operate the mouse, and how to move around the text and use menus to find specific parts. Allowing them time to play and explore is one key to success. Other strategies to help them become independent users include demonstrations, peer support, user conferences and nearby posters with directions.

Reading the screen. Screens are not as simple as most pages, since they often have different sections for content, instructions and navigational aids. So children need to become familiar with the conventions used to communicate various features and functions. For example, clicking on icons (small graphic symbols) is a common way of navigating, and in hypertext left and right arrow icons are often used as buttons to link the current screen to the previous and following screens. Making a class display of icons and commands will increase children's awareness of them and provide a ready reminder.

Understanding the structure of the text. An electronic text cannot be held in the hand and cannot be seen as a whole (unless it's very short). Thus children need to identify features of the software and other cues to help them develop their own mental model of its overall structure. Sometimes menus or visual maps are available to provide clues. Working with paper-based models can also enhance children's understanding of the overall structure.

Reading and working with the text. Children need to become aware that authors of electronic texts use differences in position, colour, type style and font within various sections of the written text to convey messages about the content. In addition, screen-based texts are often briefer and more modular than paper-based linear texts, and they do not offer the same opportunities for highlighting, underlining or writing notes in the margin. Teachers need to prepare children for electronic texts and encourage reflection about them, just as they do with paper-based texts.

CREATING ELECTRONIC TEXTS

Selecting the appropriate media. Children need to work with a range of media and text types for a variety of purposes and audiences. They also need opportunities to make their own choices about which media and text types to use, besides being directed by the teacher. Within this framework the appropriateness of particular choices should be discussed and made explicit, either when children are using texts they or other authors have created, or when they are at the planning stage of a writing task.

More general discussions about the advantages and disadvantages of paper-based and electronic media are beneficial as well. Younger children might weigh the advantages of the portability and permanence of paper-based narratives against the attractions of the interactive possibilities offered by some computer-based narratives. Older children might consider reader responses to their texts — readers can underline, highlight and annotate paper-based texts, whereas they can modify and customise computer-based texts.

Organising the information. Many of the recognised genres of paper-based texts have parallels in electronic texts. Thus children can create procedures, information reports, explanations and arguments as computer-based texts as well as in paper form. In either case, thinking through purpose and audience will help them to decide on 'best ways' to organise information.

Electronic databases and hypertexts present somewhat different environments. Nevertheless it's equally important for teachers and children to be clear about the purpose and audience for these texts before they decide on an overall structure. In working with databases, for example, if a major purpose is to create a collection that can be easily sorted and searched for trends and patterns, entries in the key fields should be numbers, measures (using standard units), or a limited set of labels (e.g. 'black, brown, blonde or red' for hair colour). This requirement can lead to much discussion about which labels or units to use (e.g. selecting a common unit of measure to describe the mass of an elephant and a mouse in a collection of animals). However, if the purpose for creating the database is to provide information reports about a variety of mammals that can be easily browsed and searched for specific facts, then entries in fields can include rich descriptive phrases and sentences describing physical features.

Allowing time for revising and refining the text. Children will most readily spend time and effort improving the quality of their texts (whether paper-based or electronic) if they have a strong sense of purpose and audience. Attention to content, organisation and use of language conventions remains fundamental in electronic texts, but the technical aspects of presentation may add a further dimension. In hypertexts, for example, links and buttons may not work as intended, or they may be omitted so that readers find themselves 'trapped'. The term 'debugging' is often used to describe the process of trialling and refining a computer-based text until it works.

Two features of electronic texts affect the process of creating and refining them. Firstly, the screen is more public than paper, and often passers-by become an informal audience as they comment on the developing text. The public nature of the screen also contributes to the tendency for most writers to combine editing and composing when they are writing with word processors or within more specialised programs. Indeed, Cochran Smith (1991) suggests that increased attention to surface editing during the composing stage is one of the key defining characteristics of writing with a word processor.

Secondly, once a paper-based text is published in the classroom, audience response rarely leads to further revisions. Publication is equated with 'finished'. With an electronic text, however, the publishing stage (i.e. making it available for the general audience to use) does not carry the same degree of permanence. Audience response can lead to continuing refinement — in fact some writers may need help to declare their writing 'done'.

How can we use electronic texts as sources of information?

LOCATING INFORMATION

Using electronic library catalogues, factual texts and reference works involves specific skills beyond those associated with reading any section of text, and children need a variety of lessons and experiences using the different types of searching systems that exist. Most electronic texts or catalogues depend on one or more of the systems described below.

Menu-driven indexes. These involve a hierarchical approach to topics. In order to use them, children need to have some knowledge of the topic they are working on and an appreciation of its conceptual framework. For example, if they are searching a menu-driven, topic-based system for information on insects, they need to know which pathway to take when presented with the following choices:

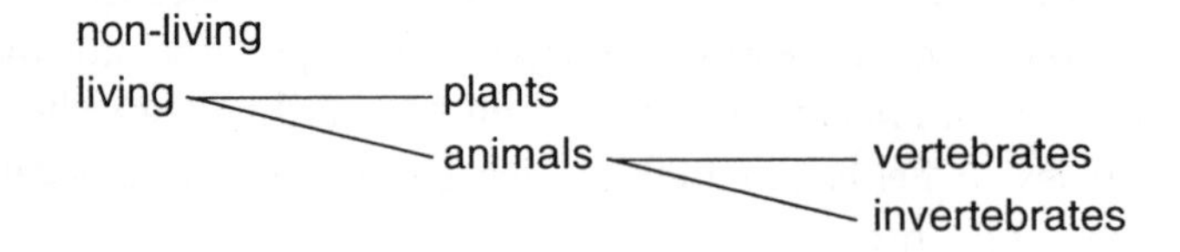

The option of browsing, familiar from paper-based texts, would not be useful because of the size and complexity of the collection.

Keyword searching in selected fields (e.g. title or subject). For successful use of these systems, children need to be familiar with the kinds of terms that might be used to describe the phenomena they are looking for. Some systems help to scaffold the searching process by providing a list of possible terms in response to a word keyed in by the user, who then selects a term from the list. Brainstorming possible terms and developing concept maps around key terms are helpful strategies to prepare children for using this type of system.

Free text searching. This involves finding all documents or sections of the text that contain an occurrence of a specific word. Some systems provide a result list indicating the number of occurrences of that word within a specified document or section (valuable information for users trying to select the most appropriate text). Children need to have many experiences of using this type of searching system; it has no parallel in paper-based systems and its power can create confusion with the sheer number of alternatives it presents.

Using connectors such as 'and', 'or' and 'not' to expand or limit searches. Most computer-based searching systems provide the user with the opportunity to refine a search by either expanding or limiting the search criteria. The common words 'and', 'or' and 'not' are often used for this purpose, and while they present little difficulty to young children in everyday contexts, their technical meanings are difficult to grasp and in some cases run counter to everyday usage.

AND is used to limit searches. The search combination 'trees AND Australia' restricts the search to portions of text that include *both* of these terms. While there might be 8 references which match the term 'trees' and 20 which match 'Australia', there will be less than 8 references, and maybe only 1 or 2, which include both terms.

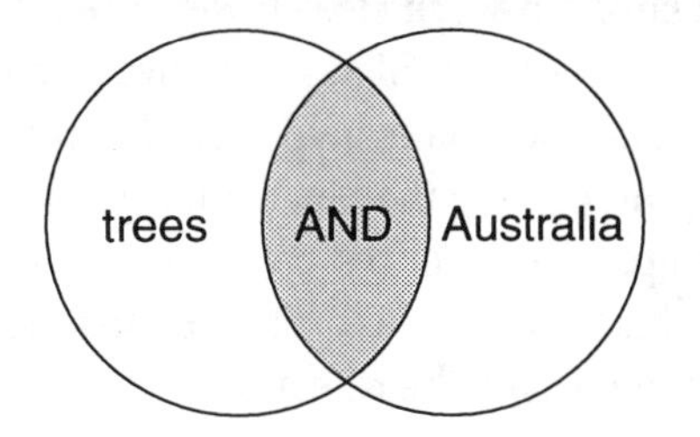

OR is used to expand searches. The search combination 'dogs OR wolves' expands the search to portions of text that include *either* of these terms. If there are 14 references that match the term 'dog' and 5 that match 'wolves', there will be between 14 and 19 references which have either term.

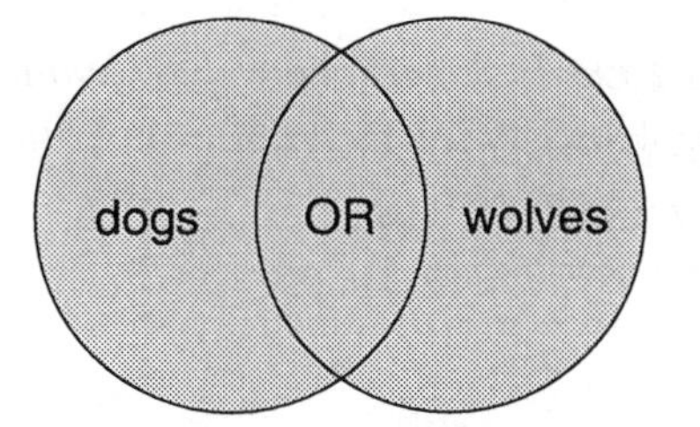

NOT is also used to limit searches, and it is perhaps the most difficult connector of all for young children to understand. The search combination 'animals NOT mammals' restricts the search to portions of text which include the term 'animals' but not the term 'mammals'. NOT is required when there are more than two alternatives involved in the search (e.g. in this case, birds, fish, reptiles, etc.), but only one possibility needs to be excluded.

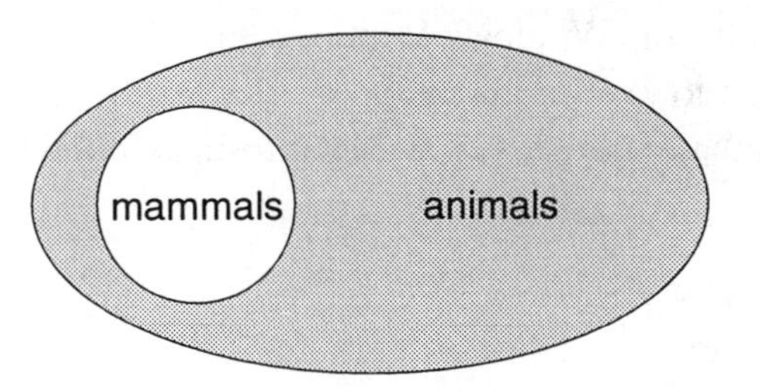

When there are only two alternatives, the positive form of the search is more appropriate — for example, 'vertebrates' rather than 'animals NOT invertebrates'.

CONTROLLING THE 'COPYING' PROCESS

Electronic cutting and pasting is a very simple process that can be used to automate the common practice of manually copying text from reference books. As more children gain access to electronic encyclopedias and word processors, there is a danger that this practice of 'copying chunks' will be further exploited. Most opportunities occur when projects are ill-defined, the source of the information is mainly prose and the project is to be presented in prose form as well. Developing strategies to ensure that children work closely with the information and convert it into other text types, such as notes, tables, time-lines and concept maps, will limit their scope for copying and substantially help them to understand the material they are dealing with. Cutting and pasting the text from the source into a word processor can be seen as the first step. Then children can delete, add, change and restructure the text on the word processor as needed. The key factor, as always, is having an authentic purpose and audience for the research.

For further reading, viewing or playing

Books and articles

Lodge, J. (ed.) 1992, *Computer Data Handling in the Primary School*, Taylor and Francis, Philadelphia.

Moursund, D. & Yoder, S. 1993, *Problem Solving and Communication in a Hypercard Environment*, International Society for Technology in Education, Eugene, Oregon.

Yankelovich, N., Meyrowitz, N. & Van Dam, A. 1985, 'Reading and writing the electronic book', *Computer*, vol. 18, no. 10, pp. 15–29.

Videos

Fostering Enquiring Minds 1985, Sydney University Television Unit, Sydney. Deals with the use of databases.

Software

DATABASE CONSTRUCTION

Bank Street Filer (Apple II).
ClarisWorks database module (DOS, Macintosh, Windows).
File Maker Pro (Macintosh, Windows, Windows 95).
Microsoft Access (Windows, Windows 95).
Microsoft Works database module (DOS, Macintosh, Windows).

Hypercard (Macintosh).
Hyper GASP (Macintosh).
Hyperstudio (Macintosh, Windows Macintosh/Windows CD ROM).
Linkways (DOS, Windows).
Macromedia Action (Windows).

ELECTRONIC ENCYCLOPEDIAS (CD ROM)

Cartopedia (Macintosh/Windows CD ROM).
Compton's Interactive Encyclopedia (Windows CD ROM).
Microsoft Bookshelf (Macintosh/Windows CD ROM).
Microsoft Encarta Encyclopedia (Macintosh, Windows CD ROM).

ELECTRONIC FACTUAL TEXTS (CD ROM)

A Tree through the Seasons (Macintosh, Windows).
A World of Plants (Macintosh, Windows).
Birds and How They Grow (Macintosh, Windows).
Butterflies (Macintosh, Windows).
Dinosaurs (Macintosh, Windows).
Magic School Bus Series (Macintosh/Windows CD ROM).
Oceans Below (Macintosh/MPC CD ROM).
Our Earth (Macintosh, Windows).
The Human Body (Macintosh, Windows).
The Way Things Work (Macintosh/Windows CD ROM).
Whales (Macintosh, Windows).
What Air Can Do (Macintosh, Windows).

Multimedia Texts

In earlier chapters the term 'multi-modal texts' has mostly been used to describe paper-based texts that communicate by combining print, images and graphic design. In this chapter the term 'multimedia texts' will be used to describe electronic texts that communicate by combining written words, images and sounds. Historically the term referred to audio-visual presentations incorporating slides, film and soundtrack. Today, however, most multimedia presentations are computer controlled or generated.

Computer-based multimedia texts are commonly found in business presentations and training and educational programs, in information kiosks at such places as museums and shopping centres, and in electronic games and books. They vary from presentations which the audience views with little or no control over pacing, to electronic stories that still have a definite sequence but allow the user to stop on a 'page' and listen to a reading of the written text or click on various graphics to trigger an animation, through to fully interactive programs where the user controls when, where and how to interact with the text. An example of the latter might be a CD ROM-based encyclopedia, where the user can choose either to browse or to search for a specific piece of information (written text, images or sounds), or an adventure game, where written text is combined with images and sounds to provide information and create situations to which the user can choose to respond. Most interactive programs use multimedia in a hypertext environment (see Chapter 7). The term 'hypermedia' has been coined to describe these types of texts, and it can be applied to any hypertext that allows for the integration of images and sounds with written text.

CD ROM technology is largely responsible for low-cost multimedia software finding its way into schools. The fascination with watching animations and video sequences and listening to recordings at the computer has ensured its popularity with children and teachers alike. At the same time, there is much hype in the popular press about the potential for multimedia to revolutionise learning. Some of this is based on convincing evidence that multimedia training programs have proved very successful and cost-effective with trainees such as pilots and engineers, and with adults learning foreign languages. To date, however, there is little to suggest that this success in an adult training environment would transfer to classroom learning. Nevertheless the number and range of multimedia texts now found in schools, homes and the wider community has created a literacy challenge for English teachers as they help children to develop the skills and understandings necessary to be confident and critical users (readers) and creators (writers) of multimedia texts.

While creating multimedia texts for commercial and professional purposes still requires professional expertise and access to sophisticated equipment, there is a range of reasonably priced software well suited to the creation of multimedia texts in classrooms. This software generally falls into two groups. Presentation software allows the creators to make a 'slide show' (a linear sequence of screens that can be played back with manual control or automatic timing for switching slides). The other alternative is hypermedia software, which allows the creators to link a collection of screens, documents and other programs in a variety of non-linear formats (see Chapter 7 for some examples).

In both cases creators can work with written text, images and sounds. The range of images includes photos, illustrations, diagrams, symbols, maps and graphs. Some images can be created at the computer in the form of line drawings or paintings (where colour is used to fill, shade and provide texture); some can be taken from an existing clip-art or photo library. Electronic cameras and scanners, which have recently been making their way into primary schools, allow children to take photos that can be directly downloaded into the computer, or to scan in line drawings, paintings or photos from paper-based originals. Images of three-dimensional objects can also be scanned with special equipment. In addition, some multimedia packages can handle animations and videos, but special software is needed to create (or digitise) and manipulate the sequence of images.

A wide variety of sounds can be used in multimedia texts. They include sounds recorded through a microphone and saved in digital form, such as voice, environmental sounds, sound effects created by children, and music performed by children or replayed from an audio cassette or similar source. Using a special device known as a MIDI synthesiser, sounds can also be digitally recorded directly from electronic keyboards or other electronic instruments. Digital sound libraries are another source; in this case children select, copy and paste the sound sequence into their multimedia text.

Note, however, that working with images and sounds requires the same concern for copyright and plagiarism as that more commonly directed towards written language. Teachers and students need to know when they can use other people's work (e.g. clip art or sound libraries) and how to acknowledge the source of what they use. Where possible, children should be encouraged to use their own images and sounds, just as they are expected to use their own words.

The simplest multimedia-making environment is usually presentation-type software, but there are a number of simple yet powerful hypermedia authoring programs which are suitable for primary-aged children. Whichever is chosen, teachers need to carefully consider the literacy challenges involved and select one focus for the task. For example, children might be familiar with written text and images but need to be introduced to some of the key issues and skills of working with sounds (e.g. the skills of recording, or an awareness of the ways to create mood with music). In such situations, models, demonstrations and joint constructions would focus on the role and relationship of sound to images and written text. Given this kind of support, children can maintain sufficient control of the processes to keep sight of the purpose and audience for the text.

Both the classroom stories in this chapter show teachers and children using inexpensive or borrowed equipment to create powerful multimedia texts. However, the secret of their success lay not in the equipment, but in the strong sense of purpose and audience which they shared.

Talking books

In the following classroom story, the teacher and children use a piece of hypermedia authoring software called *Magpie*. It is a very simple yet sophisticated program that children can master with relative ease. In some ways it is similar to the *Hypercard* program featured in Chapter 7; the main difference relates to the ease with which users can manipulate images and sounds. As with most hypermedia software, the basic units in *Magpie* are screens and buttons. Authors can place still images, text and buttons on any screen. Buttons are used to link the screen to sounds, videos and other screens.

Separate software is needed to generate the sound and video files but not to 'play' them within *Magpie*. In the story below, an *Oak Recorder* kit is used to generate the sounds. The kit comes with software which needs to be loaded onto the computer, and a microphone with a cable that connects it to the printer port at the back of the computer. With this equipment sounds can be recorded and saved as files. Once the sound is captured, it can be edited — sections can be cut out and extraneous sounds removed. This feature can be used to remove the unwanted explosive noise that often accompanies children's initial 'p' and 't' sounds, as well as the false starts and long pauses that are a natural part of the recording process. It is a very useful feature in classrooms, where the need for repeated recordings would take up valuable time. Once the sound files are saved, they can be accessed from *Magpie* by placing a sound button on the appropriate screen and linking it to the sound file.

Classroom story

Denise had been using computers in her classrooms for several years, and she had an Acorn computer in her room of eight- and nine-year-olds. During the final term of the school year, she decided to add the creation of a multimedia text to the more usual responses that the children made to the literature they read. She planned her unit of work to culminate in groups of children each creating a talking book version of a further chapter to the popular big book by James Reece, *Lester and Clyde*. Each group's work would be shared with the whole class and with other children in the same grade.

As neither Denise nor the children had used this type of software before, the technical side of the task was kept as simple as possible. Their chapters would incorporate both written and spoken text supported by illustrations, and would be presented on a sequence of screens (pages). Many of the children had never spoken into a microphone before or heard their recorded voices on a computer, and so there was much excitement and strong motivation to take special care with the spoken text.

The children had been working with *Lester and Clyde* for several weeks, exploring the text and investigating various interests in frogs, conservation and pollution which had emerged from their responses to the story. They pursued these interests in a range of other narratives and factual texts, particularly about frogs. Denise also did some extended work with the characterisation of Lester and Clyde and the types of conversations they might have had, which led to a revision of the conventions of bubble speech and ways of recording direct speech within a narrative.

The initial work with the further chapter was a whole class activity, with Denise having the children predict what might happen next. They began with a close look at the final pages, trying to identify clues about the future from the illustrations and the written text. Denise challenged the children to imagine what they might see if they came back to the pond after a few weeks. When responding to the children's ideas, she steered them towards descriptions of the scene as well as possible explanations of how it came to be that way. Next she challenged them to imagine what sounds they might hear, and what conversations Lester and Clyde might be having. She then had the children break into pairs and role play some of these conversations. When they were all back together again, some pairs volunteered to replay their conversations in front of the whole group. Denise ended this part of the session with some spontaneous productions of the sounds they had suggested, and a discussion about what they could use apart from their voices to mimic some of the sounds. Children returned to their desks with a prepared worksheet to record their selection of images, sounds and conversations.

In a later lesson children worked in groups of three or four and agreed on a scene, sounds and conversations. Each group discussed a storyline and created a narrative which had complication and resolution stages appropriate to their scene. In a whole class lesson Denise demonstrated ways to integrate Lester and Clyde's conversations into the text. Each group then drafted their final version.

In addition, art activities were undertaken to develop a variety of scenes of the pond area consistent with each group's storyline. Groups rotated between drawing

Denise and the children discuss possible futures for the pond.

and painting on paper and using a computer-based paint program, *Kid Pix 2*. Denise demonstrated how to use the program to create an oval shape and flood it with colour to make a pond; the children then added graphics from the program and their own drawings to add detail to the pond and background scene. In music, the groups created a variety of soundscapes depicting the fate of the pond, which Denise helped them to record on paper as performance scores. They played and edited their scores until each group had refined both score and performance.

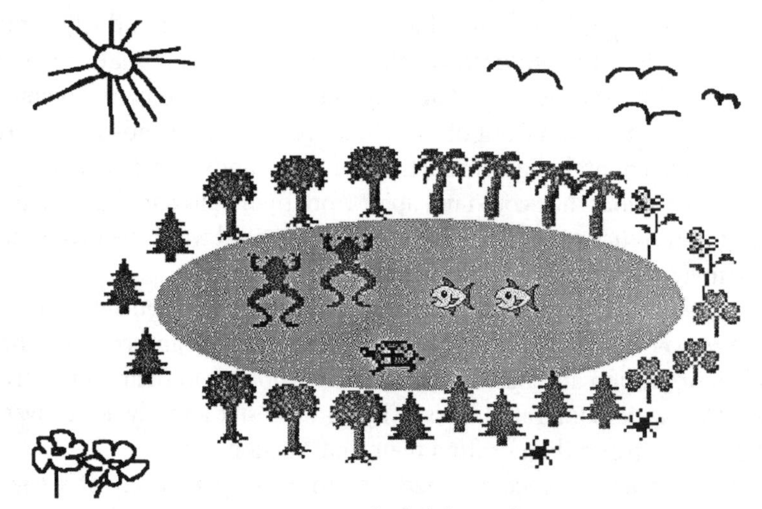

Lester and Clyde's pond.

As Denise didn't want the technical side of the process to overwhelm the creative side, she gave a number of class demonstrations and worked with one group at a time to help them use the *Magpie* software and the *Oak Recorder*. The children had also had practice using cassette recorders earlier in the year. Each group created their 'talking book' by reading their story straight into the computer using the *Oak Recorder*. They then listened to the recording and edited it where necessary, learning much in the process. They found that they had to talk slowly and precisely; they also found that since the volume on the computer wasn't very loud, they had to eradicate all background noise — quite a feat for excited eight- and nine-year-olds! It took quite a while to complete the whole task. The children had to decide who would read each section and then rehearse. Before they could record their voices onto the computer, they had to type in the text and edit it, placing page-turning buttons and sound buttons on each page. Clicking on the sound buttons would turn the recording on and off.

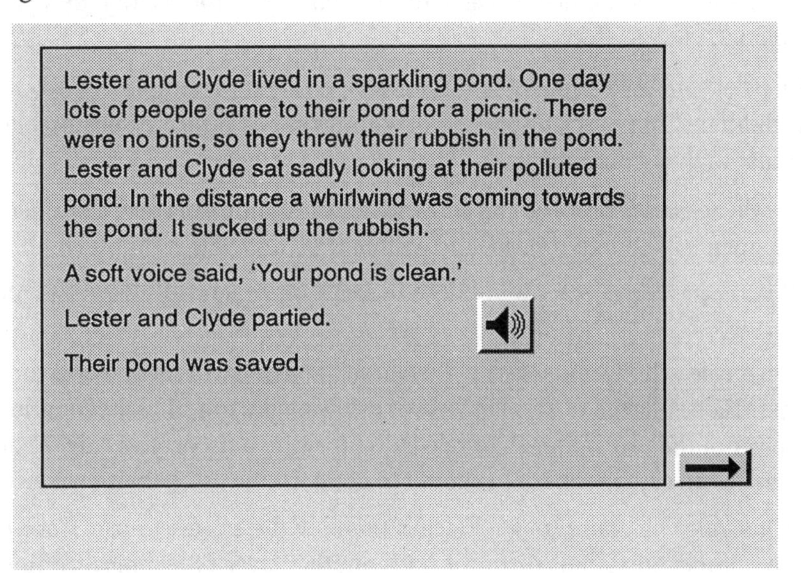

An example of one group's text, showing sound and page-turning buttons.

The final stage was for each group to add their saved picture to a separate page and use the *Oak Recorder* to record their sounds as an accompaniment. Groups rehearsed and performed their edited soundscapes, while other class members held the microphone and operated the software. Afterwards each group placed a sound button on their scene.

As always when something new is tried, Denise was continually adjusting her timetable and plans as new needs and crises emerged. Several children quickly became 'expert' users of the program and were able to act as tutors to other groups. When the final versions of texts were completed, each group proudly presented their text to the whole class, other classes, the principal, parents and any passers-by — such was the enthusiasm of the children for their work.

Trying it out

- Allow yourself time to become familiar with the software and equipment needed to work in multimedia. Check out the key features.
  - Simplest images are ones children draw themselves within paint programs; these can be copied into most multimedia programs if paint tools don't exist within the multimedia program itself.
  - Microphones are needed for recording sounds. On some computers any microphone can be plugged into the 'audio in' port, while others need a special microphone kit such as the *Oak Recorder*. Some more recent models of computer come with built-in or attachable microphones. Work out how to operate the record facility inside the multimedia software or the special sound recording software. Check to see if sounds can be edited; otherwise re-recording is the only option.
  - Find out what tools are available for written text — fonts and type styles, sizes, colours, special effects.
- As part of your own familiarisation process, create some simple examples to show the children. Commercially produced multimedia texts are often unsuitable models because of their complexity.
- Carefully select the purpose and audience for the multimedia text. Consider the text components — sounds, images and written text. Start with a simple combination.
  - What type of text will the children be creating — a recount, an explanation, a narrative?
  - What role will the images play — what relationship will they have to the written text? Help children to develop ways of using images to add to the communicative power of the text rather than relegating them to a decorative role. Avoid over-reliance on clip art; children should be comfortable using their own artwork.
  - What role will sound play? Voice is possibly the easiest to use, since creating environmental sounds or music adds another layer of technical complexity to the task.
- When you are planning learning sequences, work backwards from the product. Consider what skills and understandings the children need to create the text, and what outcomes you will draw on from the English, Art and Music curricula. In Denise's classroom, for instance, much time was devoted to children rehearsing their reading of the written text, working on pace, expression, fluency and volume. Also consider outcomes related to the design process and the 'using information technologies' strand of the Technology curriculum.
- Consider what parts of the production process the children will be involved in. You may find your first attempt more manageable if groups of children work on component parts and then combine these for a whole class text, rather than all children or all groups creating their own.

- Consider who needs to be able to operate the equipment and the software. Consider too the role of whole class and small group demonstrations, the use of tutors from older classes, and the training of some children in the class as troubleshooters.
- Build extra time into your unit of work — the first attempt at creating a multimedia text is bound to take longer than you think.

Using multimedia to persuade

The following classroom story features teacher and children creating a multimedia presentation by using *Kid Pix 2*, a program which consists of a number of modules. Its paint/draw/sound module is simple enough for use by children as young as three, yet powerful enough for older, more experienced users to create sophisticated screens combining written text, images and sounds. The slide show module allows users to create a sequence of screens which can be played back with manual control (press the space bar to go to the next screen) or with automatic timing for each slide.

The slide show module contains a variety of tools to support the building of a presentation. It uses delivery vans as a metaphor for each slide to be included. The four main tools (visible at the base of each van in the picture below) are 'pick a picture', 'pick a sound', 'pick a transition' and the 'time slider'. These allow users to add a saved picture to a particular delivery van to create a slide, add sound to the slide, choose a visual effect to accompany the transition to the next slide, and decide on the length of time that the slide will be displayed on the screen. The added sound plays automatically once the slide is displayed. The duration of the sound needs to be matched to the time that the slide is on view, so that the whole sound recording may be heard.

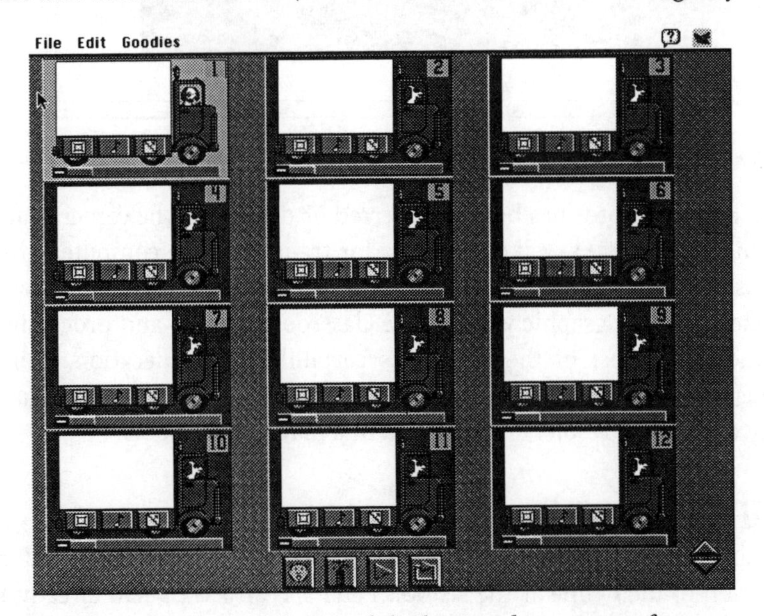

A screen from the slide show module showing the sequence of screens.

The order of slides can be edited by 'dragging' one of the delivery vans to a different position on the screen. At the bottom of the screen there is a facility for correcting mistakes, as well as 'play' and 'play loop' buttons so that creators can view their show as they are building it. The completed slide show can be saved either as a regular presentation on the same computer, or as a self-running show that can be used on other computers even if they don't have *Kid Pix* software loaded.

The children in the following story included photos in their presentation, as well as images created within *Kid Pix 2*. The photos were taken with *Quicktake 100*, a special camera that stores pictures in its memory as digital information. Connecting the camera by cable to the computer allows the stored pictures to be downloaded into software that comes with the camera. From there the pictures can be copied into paint/draw programs such as *Kid Pix 2*. The quality of the screen-based photos is dependant on the resolution of the monitor and the number of colours that the paint/draw program can access.

The photos are directly downloaded to the computer for viewing and saving.

When a set of photos has been transferred or discarded, the camera can be reset to take more photos. As well as allowing for transfer to the computer, this type of camera solves two problems that teachers commonly encounter when they undertake any photographic work in the classroom — cost and processing delays. While the initial cost of the camera is certainly a consideration, children can experiment, practice and discard any number of photos without additional expense, and they can see the results of their work in a matter of minutes.

Classroom story

Each year in Peter's school the graduating classes (Year 6) present a gift in appreciation of their time at the school. Peter's Year 5 class had already begun to consider what they might do the following year. They had been discussing a rather

Peter and the children inspecting the site.

ambitious project of creating a small native flora and fauna reserve in an area with a cluster of established eucalypts near the school boundary. (As the school is located in a new housing development, there are few established trees, parks and gardens in the neighbourhood.) Peter decided that the children's interest in the topic could be the basis of a major unit of work drawing on outcomes from several areas — Science, Environmental Studies, Technology, English, Maths, Art and Music. The main thrust of the work would involve developing a proposal to put to the other Year 5 classes, the school executive and the parent support group. The proposal would include a rationale for having a reserve, a design of the reserve, the estimated cost and a time-line of the work.

With the encouragement and support of the school's computer coordinator, Peter decided to include the use of multimedia presentation software in the unit. He had a Macintosh computer in his classroom and was familiar with the paint and sound recording features of *Kid Pix 2*. However, he had not used the slide presentation features before, and while he was familiarising himself with them, he saved some of the examples he created to show the class at a later date. Several children became fascinated as they watched Peter practice before school, and they were soon offering him advice and experimenting with the same features themselves at other times. Three children who had *Kid Pix 2* at home were so excited by what they saw Peter doing that they worked with their own software and soon became class experts. Peter also took time out to learn to use the digital camera which the school had borrowed from the local resource centre. Again the children soon became the experts and were keen to use 'out of class' time to take photos of each other and almost everything else in the school!

The viability of the project had already been checked with the school principal, and invitations were issued to a number of experts to view the site and talk to the class. They included the school's general assistant, who had earlier created a number of native flora gardens in the school, an officer from the local field studies centre, a parent with expertise in native plants, and an officer from the parks unit at the local council. Selected children videotaped each presentation, while others took notes; these records would be used later as sources of information. Over the next few days children brainstormed as many ideas as possible and invited the principal in to talk about her views on the project.

Next Peter shared with the class his ideas about how they would proceed over the following weeks. A great deal of discussion ensued, and it was finally decided that the task of developing a proposal for the nature reserve would be divided into four modules:

1. Developing a rationale for the project.
2. Designing a nature reserve.
3. Preparing a costing and time-line.
4. Designing an advertising and fundraising campaign.

Peter subsequently made a plan for each of the modules. The first two would be worked on simultaneously, as would the last two. Each child would have a role in both sets.

Module 1

Goal

To develop a rationale for the establishment of a reserve within the school grounds.

Strategies

1. Interviewing other students in the school, members of staff and a number of parents.
2. Further examining the ideas presented by the outside experts.
3. Reading reference materials on urban conservation, nature reserves, etc.

Outcome

A one- to two-minute multimedia presentation of the rationale.

Peter's plan for the multimedia module.

The first module began with groups of children being assigned tasks for collecting information from the various sources nominated in Peter's plan. As the children had never before combined sound, images and written text on the computer, Peter had decided that the multimedia presentation of the rationale would be created as a teacher-directed joint construction. He used the saved examples from his own experiments with *Kid Pix 2* as models for the children. The salient features he emphasised were the need for a tight and logical sequence incorporating an introduction, a series of reasons and a conclusion, and the need for a persuasive feel to the presentation overall.

Peter next introduced the notion of 'storyboarding' as a way of recording the sequence of ideas in sounds, images and written text. As the key ideas were placed in order, he encouraged the children to think about what sounds and images and written text would support them. The following were suggested:

- some examples of comments from other children in the school (voice)
- some pictures of what the area looks like now (photos) and what it could look like (photos and sketches)
- some recordings of birds from other nature reserves (sounds)
- some pictures of the plants that could be used and birds that might visit the area (photos or line drawings)
- a summary of the reasons in point form (written text)
- a speech presenting the rationale (voice).

As a whole class they constructed a first draft of the storyboard. Each group was given a photocopy and time to discuss other possibilities among themselves. The groups were also responsible for seeking advice from other people in the school about what should be included. Another whole class session saw the children vigorously presenting their ideas. Some who had become *Kid Pix 2* experts had already created several example screens based on the storyboard and demonstrated their pages to support their points of view. In particular they were able to show that several of the ideas about including photos needed to be tested out before final decisions could be made. Their concern was based on the poor quality and lack of clarity in some sample photos.

At this point Peter revised his time schedule and allocated a week for all children in the class to have the opportunity to take photos and create screens. He devoted some class time to improving photographic skills and also negotiated the occasional use of two computers elsewhere in the school to relieve the pressure on his own. As groups of children finished their screens, they were all incorporated into a slide show called 'Ideas', which Peter used as the basis for a class discussion about the final design of the presentation. Groups then worked to refine each of the selected screens, create new ones, take photos and work on an overall script. In order to make the task more manageable, Peter reorganised the afternoon timetable so that half the class could work on the projects, while half continued with other class work independently.

Each afternoon session began and finished with a whole class discussion about what had been accomplished and what needed to be done, so that everyone was kept informed about the progress of the project. This system worked smoothly enough until they began to run out of space on the hard disk of the computer because of the

Photographers at work.

large amounts of memory occupied by the files of sound and images. With the computer coordinator's help, the problem was solved by deleting unwanted earlier versions of files and arranging to temporarily swap Peter's computer for another in the school with significantly more memory.

While all this was going on, Peter took the opportunity to have a whole class discussion about condensing the script. It was decided that they would avoid duplication between the written and spoken texts as far as possible, and that they would record bird calls to insert between segments of the spoken text (some children had suggested that periods of silence would be boring).

When Peter felt the class had the first module under control, he introduced the second, the design module, and allocated a number of tasks to individuals and groups. Help was sought from parents to accompany small groups of students to other nature reserves and retail gardening outlets, and a whole class excursion was organised to the city's botanical gardens. There botanists and gardeners shared their expertise about native flora and healthy growing conditions and introduced the notion of garden maintenance. Children subsequently shifted their interest to plants that would require little maintenance but still attract a variety of birds.

Back in class the children worked on designs and identification of species they would plant in the reserve. They consulted many references from the school and local libraries, as well as countless gardening books they found in their homes. Two groups worked with the general assistant to create a basic map of the area, and the artistic talents of several children and a parent came to the fore as they produced several designs for the class to discuss.

During this phase the time had come to lay the soundtrack (voice and sounds) and select the time period for each slide in the presentation to match the sound. It quickly became apparent that the classroom was unsuitable as a recording venue because of external noise. So the computer was moved into one of the offices in the main building, and children were rostered to arrive early at school and work on the recording. These sessions seemed endless as there was no way of editing the results; whole recordings had to be repeated if there were any problems.

While this was happening before school, work was continuing on the design during class time. One of the key issues to emerge in discussion was the amount and type of unsupervised access that children might have to the planned reserve during recess and lunch. This became a vexed question (just as it does in the wider community), and it was strenuously debated until Peter broke the impasse by asking several pairs of children to phone various government organisations and conservation groups to seek advice. The final decision involved defined pathways, small walls around the garden sections, and two clearings with bench seats that would allow for 'passive' recreation. All flora and fauna would be declared 'protected', and there would be school rules about appropriate behaviour.

As the second module came to an end, Peter could sense the need for a change of pace. In discussions with the principal and the president of the parent association, it was agreed to bring forward the date of the presentation and restrict it to the rationale and designs for the reserve. The children would present these to the other Year 5 classes and to an evening meeting of the parent group, seeking their agreement in principle for the project. Much time was spent in class rehearsing the presentation, which would include a number of children talking, the 'slide show' and the unveiling of three possible designs. Peter took care to introduce the children to some of the elements of public speaking, including use of voice (pace, volume and variation) and the need for eye contact.

The presentation to the other Year 5 classes came first and was very well received. All children in the class as well as their parents had been invited to attend the evening meeting. There the project was wholeheartedly approved, and the children were buoyed by the interest and praise they received for their thorough research and professional presentation. Next day they were all euphoric, though they welcomed the notion of a few weeks' break before they began the next phase!

Trying it out

- Consider the purpose and audience of the multimedia text carefully. The complexity of the task needs to be carefully identified and matched by children's interest and involvement in the outcome.
- Consider children's previous experience and skills. Since work with written texts tends to dominate the classroom day, children may well need extra time working with images and sounds if these components are to make a significant contribution to their texts. Plan learning experiences that will enhance skills in separate media as well as in the multimedia format.
- Plan to work towards the achievement of a number of outcomes from a range of curricula, such as English, Drama, Mass Media, Visual Arts, Music and Technology Studies. Plan for a balance of outcomes in oral as well as written strands. Consider outcomes from the viewing strand of the National Statement on English — this type of work provides the ideal opportunity for children to appreciate that images are purposefully constructed.
- Check out the hardware and software available. Multimedia texts take up a great deal of memory (which is why CD ROM technology is so appropriate) and a hard disk is a necessity. Investigate how the software works. Do you need extra software to manipulate the images and sounds? What recording devices do you need? Can you borrow them from a local resource centre or high school? What other devices are needed?
- If the children will be working with a new piece of equipment, plan for extra time so that they can become familiar with it and explore ways of using it creatively.
- Take time to become familiar with the software. While you are exploring its features, create some examples to use as models for the children.
- Assess children's expertise and experience with multimedia software. Nowadays many popular retail outlets bundle software, such as *Kid Pix 2,* with computer purchases. Computers sold with CD ROM drives often come with some sort of CD ROM-based collection of non-copyright photos, as well as software to view and manipulate the images. So there's a fair chance that some children already have some expertise.
- Create a time-line for the unit of work within which you will develop the multimedia text. Identify the point in time at which the text needs to be finished. Work backwards from there, pinpointing times for creating the various components of the text, for developing the content base, and for developing the skills needed to operate the various software programs and other devices. Incorporate planned and spontaneous demonstrations along the way.
- Consider a teacher-led joint construction for the first attempt, or provide a template (screens with links, etc.) to which children can add the various elements of the

text. If the text is important yet complex, consider having the children create the individual components separately before combining them in the multimedia software with the assistance of a teacher, parent or older child.

- Share with children your reasons for selecting the various media components. Where possible, involve them in decisions (e.g. by asking, 'How could we illustrate this best? A photo? A line drawing?'). Prepare children for the time when they will need to make independent decisions about selecting appropriate media and forms of images and sounds.
- Consider limiting each group of children to just one component of the project, allowing them to develop expertise in their area. This expertise can be shared and broadened in later projects. Consider letting children contribute according to their strengths (e.g. talking, drawing, photography, writing).
- Plan access to the computer based on 'time needed to complete the task' rather than the more common 'equal time for each group'. This will allow groups to complete substantial sections of their work in one sitting. If expertise and compatible equipment are available in some children's homes, encourage them to continue working at home (just as you would with most other classroom projects).
- Monitor group dynamics and role allocation. For example, children with expertise developed at home should not be allowed to dominate the key roles or the control of equipment or technical processes.
- Consider organisational issues such as access to computers, handling sound in the classroom, and use and care of camera and batteries.
- Monitor children's work at the computer as well as away from it. At the computer look for attention to screen design features as well as cohesion between the written text, images and sounds. Consider having children keep a learning log to help them evaluate their own learning.

Issues to consider when planning to use multimedia texts

What do I need to get started?

§ A computer with a hard disk, with a reasonable amount of memory. (However, there are still a few programs around for older machines, such as the Apple IIe and the BBC, that allow you to do some simple multimedia work without a hard disk.)

§ Easy-to-use multimedia authoring software — that is, software that children will find easy to use, yet is powerful enough to create and manipulate written text, images and sounds. You need to become familiar with the software and determine if other types are needed too. For example, younger children might find it easier to create their images in a familiar paint/draw program and then cut and paste their images into the multimedia software.

§ Access to libraries of images and sounds that children can use in their texts. Remember that the source of anything they use should be acknowledged, and give priority to anything they can create for themselves.

§ Other devices and software as needed, depending on the images and sounds you wish to work with. Many of the more expensive items might be borrowed from local resource centres or high schools, or bought as a shared resource with other local schools. Such items include:
  - a scanner
  - a digital camera
  - a video digitiser
  - microphones
  - a MIDI synthesiser
  - animation software
  - video handling software
  - a projection device for large group viewing.

§ A technical support person (e.g. colleague, parent, school student with particular expertise).

§ A simple, short-term project that will be a gentle beginning, such as:
  - having children present an information report orally supported by images and text on the computer screen
  - transferring a class story from paper to screen and adding a voice which can tell the story for a younger audience
  - recounting an excursion recorded on camera and audiotape.

§ Time to plan your involvement and develop some expertise.

§ A sense of humour for when things inevitably go wrong!

Should I use multimedia texts in my reading program?

Multimedia texts have a wide range of forms and purposes. They can be fictional narratives or factual texts, linear texts or hypertexts, passive or interactive texts, or a combination of any of these. On the one hand, their complexity and variousness place fresh literacy demands on users. On the other hand, some of their sophisticated features provide scaffolding and support for a wide variety of more traditional literacy demands.

Some of the new literacy demands stem from the electronic medium and the non-linear structure of many of the texts, and these have already been discussed in Chapter 7. Other demands are directly linked to the use of sounds and images with written text, and these present teachers with two significant challenges. The first relates to the assumptions that many children (and teachers) bring to multimedia texts, which might be summarised like this: 'Images are combined with sounds and animations to decorate the text, and the interactivity makes playing with the text more fun'. Such assumptions are reinforced by a variety of experiences, including use of some of the inferior first-generation multimedia texts that reached homes and schools. In particular, a number of the early electronic narratives and encyclopedias are poor models of multimedia texts. In some narratives, for instance, the images and the ways of interacting with them are so entertaining that children's attention is drawn away from the plot and characters. Indeed, the distraction is so great that afterwards they have trouble retelling the story; they can only describe their interactions with the images. If such texts are to be included in reading programs, their use needs to be carefully monitored — not only because of this problem, but because they reinforce inappropriate notions about the roles and relationships of written text, images and sounds within multimedia texts.

The second challenge relates to the first. Children's aural and visual literacies are not as well developed as their written literacies. The notion that images can be purposefully constructed with carefully selected elements to convey specific messages is often not appreciated by children (or by adults). Nor is the power of technology to modify images and create composites — which is now so well developed that we can no longer assume that a photo or a video clip represents reality. Visual texts require the same sort of time, attention and effort that written texts usually receive if children are to develop the ability to critically 'read' the images as well as the words in multimedia texts.

Incorporating outcomes from the viewing strand of the National Statement on English, and working with the strategies and issues presented in the Queensland Education Department's *Using Visual Texts*... are helpful starting points. In addition, many Media Studies curricula and resources focus on visual literacy. However, these documents rarely consider computer-based images and their unique characteristics, nor do any of the resources begin to tackle the role of sound. Nevertheless reading programs need to provide children with plenty of opportunities to gain experience of using multimedia texts. At times the focus can usefully be on a single mode (images, sound or written text), as well as on the relationships between the three modes.

Besides providing a variety of challenges, multimedia texts have a range of features that can be used to meet a number of learners' literacy needs. They include the use of voice to support written text, access to spoken and written texts in languages other than English, easy access to additional texts to aid understanding, and access to a guide (an identifiable dramatised personality whose spoken comments and questions can guide a user through part of the text, or demonstrate the strategies and processes of using the text).

These features vary depending on the purpose and audience for the text. For example, almost all narrative electronic books designed for young children have a range of options for voice support of the written text (e.g. the option of listening to a voice read the whole story, or a paragraph, sentence, phrase or word within the text). Users can replay a selection as many times as they choose. In some cases they can select highlighting or underlining which indicates which words are being spoken. Such features can provide substantial support for the emerging reader.

Some narrative software allows users to hear translations of individual words or phrases in another language, or hear and see the whole text in another language. Access to a second language has proved particularly helpful amongst the bilingual communities in the south-west of the USA, where two languages, English and Spanish, dominate. In Australia, however, many multilingual classrooms have small numbers of children from many countries, and at present the ideal of access to many languages is not available.

For further reading, viewing or playing

Books and articles

Ambron, S. & Hooper, K. (eds.) 1990, *Learning with Interactive Multimedia: Developing and Using Multimedia Tools in Education*, Microsoft Press, Redmond, Washington.

D'Ignazio, F. 1989–present, 'Multimedia Sandbox', a regular feature in *The Computing Teacher* which discusses a range of practical issues — e.g. classroom management (1989, vol. 17, no. 3, pp. 27–28).

Gray, A. 1992, 'Multimedia: establishing new paradigms or reaffirming old skills?', *Australian Educational Computing,* vol. 7, no. 2, pp. 13–17.

Neilsen, J. 1992, 'It's more than just seeing: on multimedia and visual thinking', *Australian Educational Computing,* vol. 7, no. 2, pp. 9–13.

Preston, D. 1994, 'Multimedia projects in the classroom', in S. Wawrzyniak & L. Samootin (eds.), *Ask Me Why? Proceedings of the 10th Annual New South Wales Computers in Education Conference,* NSW Computer Education Group, Sydney.

Software

MULTIMEDIA SYSTEMS

Fine Artist (Macintosh, Windows, Macintosh/Windows CD ROM).
HyperStudio (Macintosh, Windows, Macintosh/Windows CD ROM).
Imagination Express — Destination Series (Macintosh/Windows CD ROM).
Kid Pix 2 (DOS, Macintosh, Windows).
Kid Pix Studio (Macintosh/Windows CD ROM).
Media Weaver (Macintosh, Windows, Macintosh/Windows CD ROM).
The Multimedia Workshop (Macintosh, Macintosh/Windows CD ROM).
3-D Movie Maker (Windows CD ROM, Windows 95).

ELECTRONIC BOOKS

For CD ROM encyclopedias and factual texts, see lists appended to Chapter 7; for narratives (talking books), see list appended to Chapter 4.

Using Telecommunications

Electronic communication is simply the exchange of information between computers, and it allows electronic texts to be transmitted to audiences close by or far away. The computers involved may be directly connected to each other through cables, or they may be exchanging information through modems and telephone systems. A modem is a device which enables a computer to send and receive information via the lines, microwave transmissions or satellites that telephone systems use.

Groups of computers which can exchange information are called 'networks'. Computers in a local area network are directly linked through cables. Increasing numbers of schools have local area networks for school administration and library management as well as for classroom learning (these classroom networks may be confined to one room or distributed through the school). Over large distances computer networks normally involve the use of telephone systems — a form of communication frequently referred to as 'telecommunications'. Telecommunications allow schools to belong to networks extending across their state, their country or around the world.

Most telecommunications users belong to a service which provides a range of facilities to its subscribers. There is a range of services available to Australian schools, but those most commonly used are the Telecom Nexus Information Service, operated by the South Australian Department of Education, and Keylink, operated by Telecom Australia. The majority of Australian services provide access to schools and projects in other countries. Some also provide access to the Internet, an international network that is currently attracting much attention in both the business and education sectors. The Internet is discussed more fully at the end of the chapter.

Three common classroom uses of electronic communication are electronic mail, computer conferencing, and information retrieval from databases stored in remote computers. The first of these, commonly known as 'e-mail', involves the transmission of *written* information from one user to another user or group of users. As with traditional mail, the name and address of the recipient have to be identified. Teachers can use e-mail to write to colleagues in other states or countries and share information on teaching ideas and resources. Children can write to others in distant locations and share information for a project they are completing collaboratively. In the first classroom story in this chapter, children use e-mail to correspond with a 'character' from a book they have read.

Computer conferencing uses e-mail to enable a number of users to discuss issues of common interest via a public bulletin board. Discussion begins as users post questions, ideas and information to the bulletin board and other users respond by writing back to the board. Responses can be addressed to the user who originally posted a particular notice or be intended for general reading. Usually bulletin boards focus on particular topics. On the Nexus system, for example, there are boards which focus on curriculum resources, Australian history and geography topics, and endangered species.

Users can also subscribe to discussion groups: as members they receive all mail posted to a central mail server and again can reply to all members or to an individual member who posted a particular message. There are several discussion groups of interest to English teachers on the Internet, including English teachers K-12, teachers of English for Science and Technology, and teachers of ESL. Children's groups include a literature discussion group. However, since some groups are not moderated, the quality and relevance of the discussion may vary. In the second classroom story in this chapter, children publish their writing on a bulletin board as part of a 'tele' tour of Australia.

Retrieving information from databases stored in remote computers can occur in a number of different ways. Nexus, for example, provides users with access to a range of text-based databases which teachers and students can search for the information they want. These include the *Aboriginal Studies Resource Database, Aesop's Fables,* the *Macquarie Dictionary, Dinosaurs of the World, Whales of the World,* and the *Culturally Inclusive Resource Database.*

In addition, a number of institutions and agencies have made their databases available to the general public. Using 'telnet' software, a user can make direct contact with a remote computer system, log on to the system and interact with the database (usually text-based). For example, teachers could telnet to the catalogue of a local university library and use it as if they were seated in the library using the catalogue terminal. Some classroom examples from the Internet include access to on-line space research from NASA, weather and earthquake information from international monitoring agencies, and collections of literary works.

A more recent facility for retrieving information is the Internet's World Wide Web (WWW). It is the most organised part of the Internet and the easiest to use.

The distinctive feature of this facility is that the information, which can include images, sound and written text, is linked through a hypertext environment (see Chapter 7) to other information stored on that computer or on other computers anywhere in the world. It has the potential to revolutionise information retrieval systems.

'Characters Online'

Each year an Oz Projects calendar arrives in Australian schools. Oz Projects is a collaborative program, supported by state education systems and corporate sponsors, which aims to bring a variety of high quality curriculum-based telecommunications projects to schools.

One of the many events included in the Oz Projects calendar is 'Characters Online'. It begins on an advertised date when one character from a selected narrative posts an introductory message to a bulletin board. Participating classes look up the bulletin board and read the message. They reply to the character in their own way with information about themselves, responses to the story and questions they would like the character to answer. The character then replies to each class by e-mail, answering questions and responding to information and comments made. Replies often take up to a week to arrive as the character may have up to a hundred schools to respond to. All replies to participating classes are posted to the bulletin board so that everyone else can read them.

Classroom story

Shirley teaches a class of seven- and eight-year-olds. Most classes in the school are regular users of Keylink and Oz Projects (which is available through Nexus as well as Keylink). There is a modem and telephone line permanently set up in one of the smaller, special purpose classrooms, and a laptop computer with telecommunications software which all classes can use. Each classroom also has one or two computers.

At the beginning of the year the Oz Projects calendar arrived in the school detailing all the projects for the year. In consultation with the computer coordinator, Shirley chose projects and made plans. She decided to participate in all of the 'Characters Online' and 'Talk to a Scientist' projects.

During Terms 2 and 3 the class participated in Characters Online sessions with the third pig from *The Three Little Pigs* and the troll from *The Three Billy Goats Gruff*. All writing to the third pig was based on whole class joint construction of letters and questions. During this first experience of writing to story characters, the issue of their 'reality' was confronted. Shirley found it a great opportunity to reinforce the notion that stories are 'constructed', pointing out that people were playing the role of the characters. However, her emphasis did not dampen the children's enthusiasm for the project at all; instead some of them began role playing characters from the story with each other. Correspondence with the troll included procedural texts for vegetarian recipes, in response to the troll introducing himself to the class as a highly misunderstood vegetarian. The idea for the recipes came from two children in the class who were vegetarian themselves.

In Term 4 the class corresponded with the characters Rich and Bee from the story *Imagine* by Alison Lester. The class had been working with the text for about three weeks before they received the introductory letter from Rich. They had read the book together and by themselves, and they had discussed various features of the story and the way it was presented. Shirley had found that this class really enjoyed discussing the design features of the book, such as types of illustrations, use of colour and the layout of the text. She had prepared a range of oral activities which involved the children responding to the text in some way, and a booklet of activities that would lead to a set of structured written responses to the story. One activity was to draft questions that they would like to ask Rich and Bee.

On the advertised day, Shirley took the whole class over to the room with the telecommunications set-up. The children watched as she performed the initial 'logging on' procedure. She talked her way through the demonstration, questioning and explaining at various stages. She soon found the letter on the bulletin board and the whole class read it together. A copy was saved to disk to be printed out for display back in the classroom. Shirley also planned a range of reading activities around the letter.

Posted: Wed, Sep 22, 1993 4.15 pm EST   Mes: NJJD3488-4837
From: COL.PL/OZ.PROJECTS/KEYLINK.PROMOTION
To: rich.bb
Subj: 1st letter to students

Hello everybody,
Have you seen me in the book 'Imagine' by Alison Lester?
My name is written in the book – can you find it?
My sister Bee and I dress up a lot and imagine we are in many different places.
Do you dress up?

I play lots of games with my sister. What games do you play? Can you describe how you play this? Who do you play with?

Bee and I often visit different places in our imagination. Have you visited special places in your imagination?

I am looking forward to hearing from you. My Keylink mailbox is COL.PL. You can write to me between 25 October and 15 November. Look out for my replies.

Your friend
Rich.

A copy of the introductory letter.

The following day the class discussed how they might respond to Rich and Bee. They agreed that this time they would jointly construct a class response to Rich's questions and also send a number of questions from individual children. They went back to their booklets, adding to and refining their responses and questions. Then

Shirley asked them to each bring their draft questions to a small group meeting and share what they had written. Each group chose one question from each child to be put to the whole class. In the whole class session, all the selected questions were recorded on the board and a general discussion took place. Children identified overlapping questions, interesting questions, unusual questions, questions whose answers could be found in the story, and questions to which they would particularly like to know the answers. Finally seven children's questions were chosen, and in the next session the whole class jointly refined them to this form:

Which imaginary place did you like best? – Blake
Was it fun imagining about dinosaurs? – Gryff
Was it fun being in the Imagine book? – Michael
Do you imagine any other places? – Liam
What was your favourite dinosaur and why? – Chris
Do you go to school? – Lydia
Do you imagine when you are asleep or awake? – Lucinda

Two children were selected to save these questions on a disk that also contained the class responses to Rich's questions. They took this disk over to the telecommunications computer and again the whole class came to watch as the questions were sent off to Rich and Bee. Over the next week or so the children continued their activities with the story and Shirley checked Keylink for an answer from Rich and Bee. Finally it arrived, and the class set off once more. Their excitement was evident as they read Rich and Bee's responses to their questions.

Posted: Sun, Nov 28, 1993 3:12 pm EST Msg: ZJJD 3621-8393
From: COL.PL/OZ.PROJECTS/KEYLINK.PROMOTION
To: school.p
Subject: Answers from Rich

Dear 2w,

Thankyou for writing to me through Keylink. Bee and I have been very busy answering all the questions from children around Australia.
Blake - I really couldn't choose a special place. They are all special in their own way.
Gryff - I've been imagining about dinosaurs since I first heard of them. It's such a shame they became extinct. Wouldn't it be good to have a Diplodocus for a pet?
Michael - Yes, it was fun being in the book. Bee and I visited so many wonderful places.
Liam - Lately I've been imagining space and living on the moon.
Chris - My favourite used to be Tyrannosaurus Rex because it was so powerful but since I saw Jurassic Park, I now prefer the Velociraptor. It was a very smart dinosaur.
Lydia - Of course I go to school. How do you think I learned so much about dinosaurs?
Lucinda - I imagine best when I'm asleep but sometimes I find myself imagining on those hot afternoons at school too.

From Rich

Rich's responses.

The responses were saved on the same disk as before, along with all the responses Rich and Bee had made to other participating classes, and back in the classroom multiple copies were printed. The children took great pleasure in reading and re-reading them over the next week or two and, as a fitting climax to their work on the story, they read their questions and Rich and Bee's responses at a school assembly. A booklet containing responses to other classes was placed in the reading corner and soon became a favourite.

Trying it out

Near the end of the chapter is a section answering the question, 'How do I get started?' The following steps assume that there is working telecommunications equipment in the school, an account with Keylink or Nexus, and access to technical and curriculum support as needed.

- Locate the Oz Projects calendar in your school and select the book that suits the interests of your class and will best fit into your literature/reading program.
- Check the dates in terms of your other curriculum and school commitments and the amount of planning and preparation time needed. Plan to receive the introductory letter from the character in the middle of your unit of work, so that writing questions and receiving and discussing replies can all be fitted into the time frame of the unit.
- Consider access to copies of the book. Is there a big book available? Are there enough copies for a small group, or even enough for the whole class?
- Plan your literature/reading unit and identify what outcomes the Characters Online component will add to it. Consider outcomes related to constructing responses to the character's questions, as well as those related to questioning the character. What types of questions will be asked of the character and by whom? Will questions be jointly constructed in teacher-led whole class or small group sessions, or will they be independently constructed by individuals, pairs or small groups? How will you ensure that each child makes a contribution to the questioning within the project, or across a range of projects? With younger children, consider how to deal with the issue of whether the characters are real — it's important to develop an understanding of the 'constructedness' of stories from the first years of school.
- Plan access to the telecommunications equipment. Where is it? What times of day can you use it? Can the whole class view the process of 'dialling up' the service? Who will operate the equipment — yourself, a more confident colleague, some trained older students, selected children from your own class? Who will do the daily check to see if the character has responded?
- Plan how the children's questions will be e-mailed to the character. Have children compose, edit or publish their questions using a word processor. Discuss with your resource person how to get word processing files ready for e-mail transmission (this will vary depending on the set-up and software you are using).

➤ Consider ways of maximising the opportunities for children to read and re-read the various texts produced during the project. Possibilities include classroom posters, booklets of class questions and answers, booklets of other schools' questions and answers, and mail saved on a disk that the children can load into the classroom computer and read from the screen.

Becoming information providers

'Austour' is another annual Oz Projects event advertised in the calendar sent to each school. More details are given in messages like the one below, which appear on electronic bulletin boards on Nexus and Keylink.

SUBJECT: Call For Hosts For Austour 95
FROM: henry
DATE: 13:24 2-Feb-95

!!!!!!!!!!ATTENTION!!!!!!!!!!

AUSTOUR begins on Monday 6 March.

Join in an exciting electronic trip around Australia. Participate either as a host or as a travelling school, reading host reports and corresponding with participating students from various locations across Australia.

As a Host school your commitment is to prepare a Host Locality Report and send it to the AUSTOUR.BB bulletin board one week prior to students visiting your location. This allows travellers time to read your report and be prepared with questions and comments before their scheduled visit to the Host location.

All Host schools are also travellers and are expected to participate in the tour by reading and responding to reports from other Host locations.

Hosts are required from all states if possible and an itinerary for the tour will be advertised on the AUSTOUR.BB bulletin board as soon as hosts are nominated. Comprehensive details for classroom application and Host Report layout will be unloaded to the AUSTOUR.BB within the next few days.

The current urgency is to have schools nominate to be host locations. The aim is to have host schools in Queensland, New South Wales, Victoria, South Australia, Western Australia and Tasmania. I would like to prepare an itinerary by February 22nd so the first schools have time to get their reports prepared in time to begin on the 6th March.

So NOMINATE NOW for the trip of a lifetime by sending the following details:

Name of School
Year Level
Contact Teacher

SEND YOUR REGISTRATION TO THE NEXUS MAILBOX: TRAVELOZ

Hope to hear from you soon,
Thanks
Lyn Allsop, Austour Coordinator.

Schools wishing to participate contact the Austour coordinator, who prepares and publishes an itinerary. Participating classes undertake the following activities:

- they prepare a host locality report and post it to the bulletin board a week before they are visited (report headings are listed on the opposite page)
- they spend the period when they are acting as hosts checking their mail daily, looking for e-mail from visiting schools and responding to any they receive
- they visit other locations over the four weeks of the tour, read the locality reports and send questions and comments to the host school.

As all questions and comments are sent via the bulletin board, all schools can read and discuss every other school's contributions.

Classroom story

Gary teaches a class of ten- and eleven-year-olds in a school serving a community which includes more than fifty different cultural backgrounds. English and Vietnamese are the major language backgrounds. Each morning there is a one and a half hour block devoted to language learning experiences. Three mornings a week a language support teacher, Elena, works in Gary's classroom, and on these mornings they team teach and work intensively with one small group each.

The school has made the use of computers a priority over the last few years and has been able to equip each classroom with a computer, as well as having a small computer room with general purpose and special needs facilities. The room is used by whole classes, small groups and the special needs teacher, who often works on a one-to-one basis with a number of children. The telecommunications equipment is installed in this special room, as is an extension to the school phone system. This year the school has decided to equip the two Year Five classrooms with ten computers and four printers as part of a special technology project. Next year this project will extend to the Year Six classrooms as well.

Gary has been using telecommunications for several years. He regularly confers by e-mail with two international colleagues whom he first got to know on a 'tele' world tour a few years ago. Each year he looks out for the Oz Projects calendar and selects projects that match his curriculum goals and the needs of his class. He often includes books in his literature-based reading program because they are being featured in the Characters Online schedule, and he draws some of his environmental studies from the range of activities listed in the calendar.

Last year was his first attempt at Austour. He worked with small groups of children, mainly at lunchtimes, since all activities were additions to the regular classroom language program. This year, however, he decided to combine Austour with a Society and its Environment unit on 'Why do people live in communities?', partly because both would focus on the class investigating their own and other communities. Another reason for his decision was his belief that Austour provides a mechanism for children from different communities to come closer together through personal communication. He thought that this might counterbalance the emphasis on 'differences' that sometimes emerges in children's minds as they engage in comparative studies of communities.

When planning the integrated unit, Gary used the curriculum suggestions found on the Austour bulletin board as part of his resource base. The nature and duration of the language activities were planned in conjunction with Elena. The language outcomes included the following:

- *recognises that certain text types and features are associated with particular purposes and audiences*
- *controls most basic features of written language and experiments with some organisational and linguistic features of different text types*
- *adjusts writing to take account of aspects of context, purpose and audience.*

Whilst Gary and Elena continued their literature-based reading programs, they devoted other language time to the integrated unit.

Gary began the unit several weeks before the Austour officially started. In these first few weeks children investigated three focus questions: 'What is a community?', 'Where is our community?' and 'What is in our community?' These investigations provided a sound framework for the research that needed to be done for the Austour host locality report. Key headings for the report, taken from the layout posted on the bulletin board, are shown below:

Name of locality:
Population:
State:
Distance from nearest population centre over 2 000:
Name of centre:
Shire or city:
Names of contributing children and contact teachers:
Brief history of locality:
Local geographical features: (e.g. rivers, mountains, lakes)
Local industries: (e.g. dairy farming, paper manufacturing)
Educational institutions: (e.g. primary, secondary, tertiary and the types of courses offered)
Recreational/sporting facilities:
Tourist attractions:
Accommodation:
Franchise/chain stores: (e.g. Myers, McDonalds)
Health and community services: (e.g. hospitals, child care)
Law enforcement:
Transport services: (local and long distance; include the price of fuel per litre, super and diesel)
Other: (add any other information about your locality that you would like to share with the touring schools)
Price the items on the shopping list for comparison:

Milk 2 litre	Butter 500g
Cheese 500g	Cornflakes 500g
Coca Cola 2 litre	Ice cream 2 litre

Distance and methods of transport to the next locality on itinerary and the costs per person by bus, train or air:

The official itinerary began in Queensland and then moved to New South Wales, Canberra, South Australia and Western Australia. The tourists were to spend three days in each of these locations. Three weeks before their official hosting time, the children formed six friendship groups and negotiated the report headings for which they would take responsibility. The school librarian, parents and local organisations became resources as the children collected the wide variety of information needed.

The children were familiar with information reports, and so in a whole class lesson Gary briefly reviewed their purpose, organisation and conventions. Next he introduced the children to examples of host locality reports from the previous year, pointing out some of the ways they differed from more conventional information reports (e.g. lack of a general introduction). Then he and Elena led a number of small group activities where children worked with these examples, noting and recording the important features. They also discussed the reasons for the differences between the host locality report and typical information reports.

In these discussions there was a particular focus on creating brief but interesting statements for each of the headings, so that touring schools would really enjoy their visits. As the bulletin board to which their report would be posted was a 'text-only' environment, the children couldn't use page design features to make their work visually appealing. Audience interest had to be generated from the words themselves. This restriction generated much debate among the children about what makes a report interesting. Issues dealing with both content and style were discussed: for example, 'What would the visitors find most interesting about our local area?' and, 'How can we present information about our locality so that readers really feel they want to visit?' It also generated much peer conferencing of drafts, as the children were very keen to produce interesting reports. During these writing times each of the five computers was well used; groups of children sat at the screens, composing, discussing and editing their texts.

One enterprising group prepared a number of draft statements about shops and tried them out on their peers in the other Year Five class.

Draft 1

Shops: *In the shopping centre there are many different types of shops. Many are Asian. In fact there are more shop signs in Asian languages than there are in English. The biggest shop is the Woolworths supermarket.*

Draft 2

Shops: *Our shopping centre is like most local shopping centres except that many shops specialise in selling Asian goods such as food and kitchen goods. Even Woolworths, the biggest supermarket, sells a wide range of Asian foods.*

Draft 3

Shops: *In the main shopping centre of Cabramatta there is a strong influence of Asian type shops. It is like walking through Chinatown or down the streets of Hong Kong. There is one main supermarket, Woolworths. The rest are owned by Asians and have shop names in Vietnamese or other languages.*

After listening to their peers' opinions, they sat down with Elena and jointly constructed their final version. As the construction progressed, it became apparent that the purpose of the text was shifting from one of informing visitors about the community to one of 'selling' the community — using words to create pictures in the visitors' minds so that they might feel they had really visited the shopping centre. This led to a discussion of the difference between informing, advertising, guiding travellers (as in travel guides) and retelling travels (as in books written by travellers). Elena arranged for examples of these types of texts to be collected as classroom references. The group's final version was a mixture of text types:

> ***Shops:*** *Walking down the streets of the main shopping centre is like walking down the streets of Hong Kong or Hanoi. You are surrounded by brightly coloured shop signs in many different languages. You can smell the aromas of many different types of cooking and hear the sounds of different languages. Even Woolworths, which is the biggest supermarket in our community, sells a wide range of Asian foods.*

Some of the ideas the group had put forward were subsequently discussed with the whole class, and it was agreed that where appropriate the purpose would include informing and 'selling'. The children returned to their texts to reconsider their approach. Several groups maintained their focus on informing but added interesting asides. For example, after Gary alerted the history group to the story *My Place* by Nadia Wheatley, they finalised their history in the following form:

> ***Brief History of Locality:*** *Aboriginal people from the Cabrogal tribe lived in this area for over three thousand years. European settlement began in the 19th century. The area was small farms and very different to the closely settled housing of today. After the Second World War there was a great influx of European migrants. Since the 1970s, this area has seen the growth of ethnically diverse and culturally rich Asian communities. If you've read 'My Place' by Nadia Wheatley you would be able to imagine how great are the changes that have taken place in our community!*

As groups completed final copies of their work, Gary began saving all the sections together in one word processing file, ready to post to the bulletin board. As the time for posting approached, the excitement and tension mounted, and individual children and groups helped each other with their final copies.

When the important day arrived, the whole class squeezed into the small computer room and watched as two classmates dialled up Nexus and posted their locality report to the bulletin board. While they were on-line, the children eagerly noted which other schools from their state had posted reports. During the official hosting period the following week, selected pairs of children had the responsibility of logging onto Nexus, responding to any questions or comments directed to their school and reporting back to the class.

As the starting date for their own tour approached, Gary and the children held a whole class meeting to negotiate which pairs of children would be allocated to each of the schools they were visiting on the three-week itinerary. On the mornings Elena worked in the classroom, pairs would go to the computer room to read and respond to the host schools' locality reports.

Over the touring period all children (in pairs) had the opportunity to dial up, log on, read a locality report and respond with comments and questions. Gary worked with each pair, engaging them in discussion about the report they were reading and their possible questions and comments. He also acted as a technical back-up. The reports, questions and comments were saved as files on disks which were taken back to the classroom and copied onto the hard drives of all the classroom computers. This allowed several groups of children to sit around the computers and read and discuss the various reports and responses. Elena worked with these groups, while other members of the class worked independently on other language activities.

This approach of having pairs of children read and write on-line involved a lot of organisation and time, and it tied up the phone line more than usual. However, Gary and Elena felt it provided the children with a different context for reading, discussing and writing, as well as encouraging a more spontaneous, personal and informal style of asking and answering questions. (Each pair of children placed their names at the end of their messages.) It also complemented the more structured writing process involved in publishing their locality report to a general audience, and it met Gary's original goal of creating personal links between children in different communities.

One pair who were responding to a school interstate began their message with an imaginative introduction:

SUBJECT: Sorry we're running late!
FROM: traveloz
DATE: 16:47 21-Mar-95

Hello! We are on our way but are just a little bit late. Air turbulence delayed the plane and we had to catch a later flight. Hopefully we will arrive either late tomorrow (Wednesday) or early Thursday morning. We are having trouble locating you on our maps so wonder if you could send the names of major suburban centres you are near, otherwise we might get lost again as we travel out from the airport!

From Hannah and Sushin

They were very surprised the following day to receive a fax with a map showing the route from the airport to the school!

The culminating products of the project were the children's personal travelogues of their journey around Australia. Complementing their on-line work were map work, budgeting and much research on modes of travel, as well as further information they had collected about the various localities they had visited. They used this information to make comparisons between the communities in which Australians live, indicating what is similar and different about them and suggesting why these similarities and differences exist.

Trying it out

As in the previous 'Trying it out' section, the following steps assume that there is working telecommunications equipment in the school, an account with Keylink or Nexus, and access to technical and curriculum support as needed.

- Check the Oz Projects calendar or the Austour bulletin board on Nexus and select a tour that fits in with your available time and topics. Estimated classroom time for full participation in the project (host and traveller) might range from one to three hours a week for five to seven weeks. If the bulk of the preparation for the host locality report is completed before the tour begins, children (and teachers) can better enjoy the actual tour! Newcomers to Austour would find it useful to access previous years' bulletin boards on Nexus and discuss on-line their possible degree of involvement with the tour coordinator. The e-mail address of the coordinator is published in the Oz Projects calendar and on the Austour bulletin board.
- Consider the place of the project within the classroom curriculum. It may be separate from other English language activities, integrated in a broader language context, or integrated across a range of curriculum areas. You could work with a small group, or with the whole class working in small groups. With small groups, you could tailor the project to the needs of ESL children, gifted and talented children, and children with little motivation to read and write.
- Develop a curriculum plan and outcomes for the project. The range of possible activities published on the Austour bulletin board can be used as a starting point. Plan the curriculum context for preparing the host locality report and for visiting other locations. Lyn Allsop, currently Austour coordinator, uses the following sequence when visiting a new location:
  - The report is downloaded from the bulletin board and copies are made for group sharing.
  - Finding the location on maps is the first priority, so that the children know where they are going. Atlases, road maps and touring guides are used to build up a picture of the trip.
  - The group read the report and develop their impressions of the school, students and general locality.
  - Through discussion the group establishes what sight-seeing to do and what further information they want or need.
  - A response to the host school is drafted, revised and saved on the computer, ready for e-mailing to the host school and the bulletin board (so that other travellers can read it too).
- Prepare a time-line working backwards from the published dates of the tour. While this is an unusual approach to programming, it decreases the chances that opportunities for rich language learning will be overlooked or discounted because

of time pressure. Then work with the children to develop time-lines for both aspects of the project: i.e. hosting a visit (preparing the report and responding to questions and comments) and visiting other locations (all or some of the advertised schools). As children become very disappointed if no-one responds to their host locality report, and many language learning opportunities are lost if there is no interchange, it is important to commit time to a full visiting program.

- Plan who will write the host locality report, who will respond to the questions and comments received, and who will generate questions and comments at each of the other localities. Besides individuals, a variety of paired, small group and whole class combinations are possible. Some writing can be jointly constructed with you, some independently constructed.
- Consider the various text types children will write during the project and plan to revise or introduce them as needed. On the Austour bulletin board there are copies of reports and responses from previous years which could serve as models. Travel brochures, travel guides, travel stories and documentaries can provide other models. Previously written questions and responses may illustrate a conversational style.
- Consider access to the telecommunications equipment. Will you be able to use it daily during the tour? At what times and for how long? Who will operate the equipment? Who will support you if there are technical difficulties? Will you need help to prepare the files for sending?
- Prepare the children for their involvement in the project — use examples of locality reports and responses from previous years as motivation. Remind them of the time-lines so that they remain aware of the various deadlines.

Issues to consider when planning to use telecommunications

Are telecommunications projects worth all the trouble?

Yes! ... and the technology is rapidly becoming cheaper, more reliable and easier to use.

A small number of pioneering Australian teachers have been incorporating telecommunications projects into their classroom curriculum for quite a long time. In the past they often battled with software, modems and services which were very hard to use. When telephone access was not available at the school, they would take the children's work home and use their own equipment and phone to communicate with other teachers and schools.

However, over the last ten years much has been learnt about successful telecommunications projects. A key factor in making them successful is a strong curriculum base, and the Oz Projects calendar, a cooperative project between various state systems of education, is a direct response to the need for supplying classroom teachers with a range of well-structured, curriculum-based projects.

Well-designed telecommunications projects can provide:

- electronic access to people and resources outside the classroom
- motivation for students to use language in a variety of contexts
- a wider range of audiences and purposes for reading, writing, talking, listening, researching and cooperating
- opportunities to break down classroom walls and lessen community isolation as students from different geographic regions, with different world views and experiences, communicate with each other, work together and share resources as they learn
- opportunities for students to become information providers at a national or global level
- opportunities for students to use technology for real purposes and in a way that will be increasingly common in their future lives.

Other outcomes of telecommunications projects that have recently been recognised and exploited, particularly in a number of American schools, involve the purposeful use of telecommunications by children with special needs. These projects include:

- bilingual learners writing to children with a shared first language (e.g. Hispanic children on the west coast of the USA writing to Spanish children and Spanish-speaking Chilean children)
- children who are part of a cultural minority group communicating with children from the same cultural group, either minority or majority, in other communities (e.g. Afro-American children from different school districts and states communicating with each other)
- children from poorer inner-city communities communicating and cooperating with children from a wide range of social, cultural and geographical backgrounds
- children whose spoken accent creates social and communicative barriers writing in their second language to native speakers
- children with physical disabilities communicating with other children who, because of the text-only environment, respond without any preconceived images of disability (e.g. deaf children collaborating in a project with other children who are not made aware that they are deaf).

In each of these examples, one of the key outcomes has been the increased self-esteem of the learners as the social context of their learning has changed. A number of the examples have counterparts in Australia's culturally and linguistically diverse communities.

It is true that many classroom teachers achieve similar goals without the aid of telecommunications. However, the unique contribution of the technology is the ease and speed with which children can communicate and access information beyond the school fence, within Australia and across the rest of the developed world. These features enable cross-cultural exchange and global education to become a 'lived' part of classroom learning. While the quality of the learning outcomes is ultimately dependant on the quality of the learning experiences and the teaching, the technology undoubtedly provides a means of extending the range and nature of the learning experiences available to children.

How do I get started?

- Consider what you will need:
  - a computer (of any type)
  - a modem
  - telecommunications software (see p. 147)
  - access to a telephone socket or outlet (preferably a dedicated phone line)
  - a subscription to a telecommunications service, such as Keylink or Nexus, and a budget to pay for the service charges
  - a technical support person (staff member, parent, school student with expertise)
  - a simple, short-term project that will be a gentle beginning
  - time to plan your involvement.
- Seek advice from an educator with technical expertise in telecommunications, such as your system's computer education consultant, the computer studies teacher at the local high school, a parent or a member of your local community. Their help will be invaluable in helping you sort out the type and speed of modem to buy, the best service to belong to, access to a phone line, and the setting up and testing of the equipment. John Walters, an NSW Department of School Education consultant with considerable experience and expertise in this area, strongly recommends that beginning schools consider a dedicated phone line. He argues that the initial and ongoing costs compare favourably with a standard software purchase, yet every class in the school would use this resource over and over again.
- Organise purchase, setting up and access to the necessary equipment. Decide a location for the phone socket/s that will maximise class and individual access. A small number of Australian schools now have telephone connections to each classroom, and you should certainly consider having more than one — maybe one in each building in the school. If you can only manage one, consider locating it in the library, since this is the school's information resource centre. Also consider using a laptop as the machine to connect to the telecommunications equipment. When not required there, it could be taken to a classroom and used as an extra writing tool.

- Subscribe to an appropriate service. Find out which one is commonly used in schools in your system, area or state. Some states and territories have their own service, such as Tasnet in Tasmania and Nexus in South Australia; others make strong recommendations. Nexus is available to most schools in Australia and, other things being equal, is the best one to start with. It provides access to a wide range of curriculum-based projects K-12 and an increasing number of resources, and it is continually upgrading access to the Internet. Direct access to the Internet would be of little use to beginning schools (see next section). When considering commercial service providers, check the cost structure, including cost of subscription, cost of dial-up (local or STD charges) and cost of time on-line.
- Develop some personal confidence and familiarity with the service. Work with a buddy teacher, an experienced user or your system consultant, using both e-mail and bulletin boards. If possible, arrange to take the equipment home and explore the service without the time pressure of the school day. Look out for inservice courses that focus on telecommunications.
- Select your first project. 'Easter Bunny Online' and 'Santa Online' from the Oz Projects calendar are the simplest projects; they can be completed over a very short period of time and so they are good starting points. Projects such as 'Characters Online' and 'Story Express' require a little more organisation. Collaborative learning projects, such as 'Streamwatch', are usually less structured and require commitment over a longer term. Dates for all these projects are set well in advance to give time for the necessary classroom preparation (a generous lead time is vital if language learning outcomes are to be achieved). Note that 'Penpal' projects are not good starting points as they have little structure and can be sporadic in nature.
- Develop a curriculum base for the project, looking for ways to maximise opportunities for using and learning language. As well as the obvious reading and writing opportunities, consider the role of talking and listening within the project. Most writing tasks are completed 'off-line' — i.e. before the actual telecommunications session when the prepared text is sent. Composing, editing, proofreading and saving the text to file are all part of the classroom activity. Drawing on the experience of coordinating Oz Projects, Shelley Wilkins (1994) has estimated that effective telecommunications projects are 95% high quality curriculum activity and 5% use of the technology to send, receive and retrieve texts.
- Develop a time-line for the activities. Consider access to telecommunications equipment and the lead time necessary for preparatory language activities. Work backwards when selecting a starting date if you are taking part in one of the Oz Projects — their dates are fixed. If you are working on less structured projects with interstate or overseas schools, take account of time zones and different holiday periods.
- Provide children with an overview of the project, including a time-line, so that they can make sense of the various activities they will be involved in.

- Consider the logistical arrangements for the sending and receiving of mail. When will the telephone line be available? How long will you need to be logged on? How often will you need to check your mail box? Who will provide technical backup if things go wrong? Will the whole class or a small group participate in the telecommunications session?
- Evaluate the project, especially in terms of language learning. Assess children's learning in terms of your planned outcomes.
- Plan your next project!

Why all the fuss about the Internet?

The Internet is a hot topic in today's media and in the minds of many politicians. In fact one of the Labor party promises at a recent election in New South Wales was to give all school children access to the Internet.

The Internet is almost synonymous with the ill-defined 'information superhighway', and almost as ill-defined. Basically, however, it is a global electronic network that links together many other smaller computer networks belonging to universities, governments, business and major communication services around the world. The Australian component is the AARNET, currently managed by Australian universities. Today the Internet has about 30 million users, and that figure is expected to double over the next one or two years. All the networks can communicate with each other because they share common protocols (standard and rules for sending information).

The Internet is not owned, controlled or managed by any one group or organisation. Its use is not centrally monitored, nor is its expansion planned. This apparent lack of structure, or anarchy, is a legacy of the network from which the Internet has evolved. The original idea, developed by the US military and defence industry about twenty-five years ago, was to create a national computer network that would allow research and communications to continue even if parts of the network were destroyed by nuclear attack. The main users, academic and military researchers, computing students and hackers, soon established a strong ethos and etiquette of use. Unrestricted access to resources and lack of any centralised authority were key tenets of the culture.

These tenets are double-edged. On the one hand, they have resulted in educators and students having free access to the incredible range of resources and communications available on the Internet. They allow children to be information providers alongside major agencies such as NASA, CSIRO and internationally renowned museums and libraries. On the other hand, they make it possible for the Internet to be a thriving repository for pornography and lots of trivia.

The lack of any centralised control or management has some other disadvantages for educators too. There is no central registry for e-mail addresses or resources. While new software tools are being devised all the time to make it easier to find people, organisations and resources, it is still very difficult to conduct exhaustive searches. Services come and go and are of variable quality. Nanlohy's (1995) statement sums up the Internet: 'Though it is chaotic and haphazard, it is bountiful'. In its current form, educators need both the inclination to explore and lots of time to find its jewels, or the good luck to hear on the grapevine of a 'good find'.

Despite all these concerns, the Internet remains an incredible resource for educators for several reasons:

- the number of people, organizations and countries who use it
- its ability to communicate and retrieve images, sounds and text
- the number and range of resources that users can access free of charge
- the existence of low-cost, easy-to-use, PC-based software (Windows, Macintosh) to access the many resources available.

About twenty schools in the ACT have been directly connected to the Internet over the last two years through the ACTEIN Pilot Program (Huston 1994). The majority of the resulting classroom projects have been similar to Oz Projects, but with an international audience. However, two uses have been significantly different: namely, the use of computer-based interactive video conferencing as part of the schools' involvement in the Global Schoolhouse Project, and the development of World Wide Web home pages. The WWW system allows students and teachers to publish hypermedia texts using sound, images and text, and to link their 'pages' to other resources anywhere else on the Internet. These two uses are glimpses into the future!

For further reading, viewing or playing

Books and articles

Bell, S. & Scott, I. 1987, *The Electronic Classroom*, Nelson, Melbourne.

Harris, J. 1994, *Way of the Ferret: Finding Educational Resources on the Internet*, International Society for Technology in Education, Eugene, Oregon.

Huston, M. 1994, 'The Australian Capital Territory Education Information Network: ACTEIN Pilot Program Report', *Australian Educational Computing*, vol. 9, no. 2, pp. 24–28.

Williams, M. & Bigum, C. 1994, 'Connecting schools to global networks: curriculum option or national imperative?', *Australian Educational Computing*, vol. 9, no. 2, pp. 9–16.

Telecommunications software

America OnLine (Macintosh, Windows, Windows CD ROM).
Internet In A Box (Windows).
Kid Mail Connection (Windows).
Netscape Navigator (Macintosh, Windows).

Modems

There are many brands and types of modems on the market. Most modems work with most computers. You need to check that the speed (Baud rate) of the modem is compatible with the speed of the services you wish to connect to.

Services

Keylink — inquiries from all states:
Kevin McCourt
Keylink Administrator
Department of School Education
PO Box 600, Parramatta NSW 2150
Phone: (02) 561 1424
Fax: (02) 561 1128

Nexus — Coordinator, and Oz Projects Coordinator for 1995:
Henry Legedza
Nexus, LMB 12, Woodville SA 5011
Phone: (08) 243 5606
Fax: (08) 347 1781

References

The list that follows is confined to books and articles cited in the text. However, some of them also appear in the lists of recommended reading appended to each chapter, along with other titles not cited in the text.

Albert, M. & Lofts, P. 1983, *How the Birds Got Their Colours*, Ashton Scholastic, Gosford. This book is based on a story told by Mary Albert of the Bardi tribe to Aboriginal children living in Broome, Western Australia. The illustrations are adapted from their paintings of the story.

Anderson-Inman, L. & Zeitz, L. 1994, 'Beyond notecards: synthesizing information with electronic study tools', *The Computing Teacher*, vol. 21, no. 8, pp. 21–25.

Australian Bureau of Statistics 1995, *Household Use of Information Technology, February 1994*, Australian Government Publishing Service, Canberra.

Australian Education Council 1994, English: *A Curriculum Profile for Australian Schools*, Heinemann, New Hampshire.

Australian Education Council, 1994, *Technology: A Curriculum Profile for Australian Schools*, Curriculum Corporation, Melbourne.

Beaty, J. & Tucker, H. 1987, *The Computer as a Paintbrush*, Charles Merrill, Columbus, Ohio.

Blackstock, J. & Miller, L. 1992, 'The impact of new information technology on young children's symbol-weaving efforts', *Computers in Education*, vol. 18, nos. 1–3, pp. 209–21.

Cochran-Smith, M. 1991, 'Word processing and writing in elementary classrooms: a critical review of related literature,' *Review of Educational Research*, vol. 61, no. 1, pp. 107–55.

Cuban, L. 1986, *Teachers and Machines: The Classroom Use of Technology since 1920*, Teachers College Press, New York.

Elliott, A. 1994, 'Scaffolding learning in early childhood contexts', *Every Child*, vol. 1, no. 3, pp. 8–9.

Gibbons, P. 1991, *Learining to Learn in a Second Language*, Heinemann, New Hampshire.

Grunberg, J. & Summers, M. 1992, 'Computer innovation in schools: a review of selected research literature', *Journal of Information Technology for Teacher Education*, vol. 1, no. 2, pp. 255–76.

Hawkridge, D. & Vincent, T. 1992, *Learning Difficulties and Computers: Access to the Curriculum*, Taylor & Francis, Philadelphia.

Huston, M. 1994, 'The Australian Capital Territory Education Information Network: ACTEIN Pilot Program Report', *Australian Educational Computing,* vol. 9, no. 2, pp. 24–28.

Hutchins, P. 1967, *Rosie's Walk,* Macmillan, New York.

Klein, R. 1982, *Thing,* Oxford University Press, Melbourne.

Klein, R. 1982, *Thingnapped,* Oxford University Press, Melbourne.

Lester, A. 1989, *Imagine,* Allen & Unwin, Sydney.

Lieberman, D. A., Chaffee, S. H. & Roberts, D. E. 1988, 'Computers, mass media and schooling: functional equivalence in uses of new media', *Social Science Computer Review,* vol. 6, no. 19, pp. 224–39.

McCain, T. D. E. 1992, *Designing for Communication: The Key to Successful Desktop Publishing,* International Society for Technology in Education, Eugene, Oregon.

Mercer, N. 1994, 'The quality of talk in children's joint activity at the computer', *Journal of Computer-Assisted Learning,* vol. 10, no. 1, pp. 24–32.

Mike, D. G. 1994, 'Interactive literacy', *Electronic Learning,* May/June, pp. 50–54.

Munsch, R. 1982, *The Paper Bag Princess,* Scholastic, London.

Nanlohy, P. 1995, 'Not so much a highway as a very big crowd', *Information Transfer,* vol. 15, no. 1, pp. 20–21.

Nicoll, V. & Roberts, V. 1993, *Taking a Closer Look at Literature-Based Programs,* Primary English Teaching Association, Sydney.

Parker, R. & Unsworth, L. 1986, *Bridging the Gaps: Cloze for Effective Teaching,* Martin Education, Sydney.

Paterson, K. 1977, *Bridge to Terabithia,* HarperCollins Children Books, New York

Pavey, P. 1982, *Battles in the Bath,* Nelson, Melbourne.

Queensland Department of Education 1993, *Using Visual Texts in Primary and Secondary English Classrooms,* Studies Directorate (Humanities), Department of Education, Brisbane.

Reece, J. 1987, *Lester and Clyde,* Ashton Scholastic, Gosford.

Reissman, R. 1993, 'Software duos: multiple entry points for learning', *The Computing Teacher,* vol. 21, no. 3, p. 17.

Shand, C. 1994, 'The new entertainment medium: books on CD?', in S. Wawrzyniak & L. Samootin (eds.), *Ask Me Why? Proceedings of the 10th Annual New South Wales Computers in Education Conference,* NSW Computer Education Group, Sydney.

Wheatley, N. 1987, *My Place,* Kane-Miller Books, New York.

Wilkins, S. 1994, 'Making the most of OZ.Projects', in S. Wawrzyniak & L. Samootin (eds.), *Ask Me Why? Proceedings of the 10th Annual New South Wales Computers in Education Conference,* NSW Computer Education Group, Sydney.

Index

Note that page numbers set in italics refer to illustrations.